Breaking Chains

Self-help, Volume 2

Timothy Scott Phillips

Published by Arcane Horizons Publishing, 2024.

BREAKING CHAINS

First edition. November 27, 2024.

ISBN: 979-8230164968

Written by Timothy Scott Phillips.

Table of Contents

To everyone who has felt trapped in the relentless cycle of compulsive behaviors—

This book is for you.

May it serve as a beacon of hope, a source of strength, and a reminder that change is possible.

To the professionals, loved ones, and support networks who stand unwaveringly beside those in their journey to freedom—

Your compassion transforms lives.

And to the courageous souls who dare to confront their struggles—

Your resilience inspires us all.

Chapter 1: Introduction to Compulsive Behaviors

Definition and Types of Compulsive Behaviors

Compulsive behaviors are actions that an individual feels compelled to perform repeatedly, often against their own volition or best interest. These behaviors are typically driven by an overwhelming urge, leading to a temporary sense of relief or satisfaction, followed by regret or distress. The cycle of compulsive behavior can be difficult to break and often worsens over time if left unaddressed.

Compulsive behaviors fall into various categories, each with its own characteristics and challenges. Here, we'll explore some of the most common types:

1. Obsessive-Compulsive Disorder (OCD)

- DEFINITION: OCD IS a mental health disorder characterized by persistent, unwanted thoughts (obsessions) and repetitive behaviors (compulsions). Individuals with OCD often engage in these behaviors to alleviate the anxiety caused by their obsessions.

- Examples: Excessive handwashing, checking locks multiple times, and arranging items in a specific order.

2. Addictions

- DEFINITION: ADDICTIONS involve compulsive engagement in activities or substances, despite harmful consequences. Addictions can be behavioral (e.g., gambling, internet use) or substance-related (e.g., alcohol, drugs).

- Examples: Gambling addiction, substance abuse, and internet addiction.

3. Compulsive Eating

- DEFINITION: COMPULSIVE eating, also known as binge eating disorder, involves consuming large quantities of food in a short period, often accompanied by a loss of control and feelings of shame.

- Examples: Eating large amounts of food when not hungry, eating in secret, and feeling guilty after eating.

4. Compulsive Shopping

- DEFINITION: COMPULSIVE shopping, or oniomania, is characterized by an uncontrollable urge to shop, leading to excessive purchases and financial problems.

- Examples: Buying unnecessary items, hiding purchases from others, and accumulating debt.

5. Compulsive Hoarding

- DEFINITION: COMPULSIVE hoarding involves the excessive accumulation of items and an inability to discard them, regardless of their value.

- Examples: Keeping newspapers, clothes, and other items to the point that living spaces become cluttered and unusable.

6. Trichotillomania

- Definition: Trichotillomania is a disorder characterized by the compulsive urge to pull out one's hair, leading to noticeable hair loss.

- Examples: Pulling hair from the scalp, eyebrows, or other parts of the body, often resulting in bald patches.

7. Dermatillomania

- Definition: Dermatillomania, or skin-picking disorder, involves compulsively picking at one's skin, causing sores and scars.

- Examples: Picking at pimples, scabs, or other imperfections, often leading to infection and scarring.

8. Body Dysmorphic Disorder (BDD)

- DEFINITION: BDD IS characterized by an obsessive focus on perceived flaws or defects in one's appearance, often leading to compulsive behaviors aimed at fixing or hiding these flaws.

- Examples: Excessive grooming, mirror checking, and seeking cosmetic procedures.

Understanding the diverse range of compulsive behaviors is crucial for recognizing the signs and seeking appropriate help. Each type of compulsive behavior has unique triggers and manifestations, but they all share the common thread of overwhelming, uncontrollable urges that disrupt daily life.

The Impact of Compulsive Behaviors on Daily Life

COMPULSIVE BEHAVIORS can have profound and far-reaching effects on an individual's life. The impact is often multifaceted, affecting not only the person experiencing the compulsions but also their family, friends, and professional relationships. Here are some of the key areas where compulsive behaviors can cause significant disruption:

1. Mental Health

- Anxiety and Depression: Many individuals with compulsive behaviors experience high levels of anxiety and depression. The constant battle with uncontrollable urges and the associated guilt or shame can be mentally exhausting and lead to severe emotional distress.

- Reduced Self-Esteem: Engaging in compulsive behaviors often leads to a negative self-image and diminished self-worth. Individuals may feel powerless and frustrated by their inability to control their actions.

2. Physical Health

- Health Complications: Certain compulsive behaviors, such as substance abuse or compulsive eating, can lead to serious health problems. For example, substance abuse can cause liver damage, heart disease, and other medical conditions, while compulsive eating can result in obesity, diabetes, and cardiovascular issues.

- Injuries and Infections: Behaviors like skin picking (dermatillomania) or hair pulling (trichotillomania) can cause physical harm, leading to infections, scarring, and other health issues.

3. Financial Stability

- Economic Burden: Compulsive shopping, gambling, and other financially draining behaviors can lead to significant debt and financial instability. The need to fund these behaviors often results in strained resources and financial crises.

- Employment Issues: Compulsive behaviors can interfere with job performance and attendance, leading to potential job loss or reduced productivity. Individuals may struggle to maintain steady employment or advance in their careers due to the time and energy consumed by their compulsions.

4. Relationships

- Strained Interactions: Compulsive behaviors can put a strain on personal relationships. Loved ones may struggle to understand the nature of the behaviors, leading to frustration, resentment, and conflict.

- Social Isolation: Many individuals with compulsive behaviors withdraw from social interactions due to embarrassment or fear of judgment. This isolation can further exacerbate feelings of loneliness and depression.

5. Daily Functioning

- Disruption of Routine: Compulsive behaviors often interfere with daily activities and responsibilities. Individuals may spend excessive amounts of time engaging in their compulsions, neglecting important tasks and obligations.

- Reduced Quality of Life: The pervasive nature of compulsive behaviors can diminish overall quality of life. The constant preoccupation with compulsions can overshadow other aspects of life, making it difficult to find joy or fulfillment.

Personal Stories and Anecdotes

TO ILLUSTRATE THE SEVERITY and variety of compulsive behaviors, let's explore some personal stories and anecdotes from individuals who have faced these challenges.

1. Sarah's Story: Overcoming OCD

Sarah, a 32-year-old accountant, has struggled with OCD since her teenage years. Her compulsions primarily revolve around cleanliness and order. Sarah spends hours each day cleaning her apartment, washing her hands repeatedly, and checking and rechecking locks and appliances. The time-consuming nature of her compulsions has affected her job performance and social life.

Sarah recalls a particularly difficult period when she was unable to leave her apartment for fear of contamination. Her compulsions became so severe that she avoided social gatherings, and her relationships with friends and family suffered. It wasn't until she sought help from a therapist specializing in OCD that she began to see improvement. Through Cognitive-Behavioral Therapy (CBT) and exposure and response prevention (ERP) techniques, Sarah gradually learned to manage her compulsions and regain control over her life.

2. Tom's Battle with Gambling Addiction

Tom, a 45-year-old construction worker, developed a gambling addiction that nearly destroyed his life. What started as occasional visits to the casino escalated into a compulsive need to gamble. Tom began spending his entire paycheck on gambling, accumulating significant debt and jeopardizing his family's financial stability.

Tom's addiction led to frequent arguments with his wife, who struggled to understand his behavior. He often lied about his whereabouts and the extent of his gambling, further eroding trust in their relationship. The turning point came when Tom's wife gave him an ultimatum: seek help or face separation.

Tom joined a support group for gambling addiction and sought counseling. Through these resources, he learned to identify triggers and develop healthier coping mechanisms. With the support of his family and newfound strategies, Tom managed to overcome his addiction and rebuild his life.

3. Emily's Journey with Compulsive Eating

Emily, a 28-year-old teacher, has struggled with compulsive eating since her college years. During periods of stress, she would turn to food for comfort, often consuming large quantities in a short amount of time. These binge-eating episodes were followed by feelings of guilt and shame, perpetuating a cycle of emotional eating.

Emily's compulsive eating led to significant weight gain and health issues, including high blood pressure and prediabetes. She also faced social stigma and self-esteem issues, which further exacerbated her condition.

Determined to take control of her health, Emily sought help from a nutritionist and a therapist specializing in eating disorders. Through a combination of therapy, nutritional guidance, and support from friends and family, Emily gradually developed a healthier relationship with food. She learned to recognize her emotional triggers and implement alternative coping strategies, leading to improved physical and mental well-being.

4. Mark's Struggle with Compulsive Hoarding

Mark, a 60-year-old retired engineer, has been dealing with compulsive hoarding for most of his adult life. His home is filled with items he can't bring himself to discard, ranging from old newspapers and magazines to broken appliances and clothing. The clutter has reached a point where most rooms are unusable, and the living conditions are hazardous.

Mark's hoarding behavior has strained his relationship with his children, who are concerned about his safety and well-being. They have tried to help him declutter, but Mark becomes extremely anxious and defensive at the thought of parting with his possessions.

After a health scare prompted by the unsafe conditions in his home, Mark agreed to seek help. He worked with a therapist who specialized in hoarding disorder and participated in a support group for hoarders. Through these resources, Mark began to address the underlying emotional issues driving his behavior and learned strategies for gradually decluttering his home. Although the process is ongoing, Mark has made significant progress and continues to work towards a safer and more manageable living environment.

5. Linda's Experience with Trichotillomania

Linda, a 22-year-old college student, has been struggling with trichotillomania since she was a teenager. The compulsion to pull out her hair intensified during periods of stress and anxiety, leading to noticeable bald patches on her scalp. Linda felt embarrassed and ashamed of her condition, often wearing hats or scarves to hide the hair loss.

The emotional toll of trichotillomania affected Linda's self-esteem and social interactions. She avoided social gatherings and intimate relationships for fear of being judged or rejected. The compulsion also interfered with her studies, as she found herself spending hours pulling out her hair instead of focusing on her coursework.

Desperate for a solution, Linda sought help from a therapist who introduced her to Habit Reversal Training (HRT). This therapy helped Linda become more aware of her triggers and develop alternative behaviors to replace hair-pulling. With time and practice, Linda's episodes of trichotillomania decreased, and she began to regain her confidence and social life.

These personal stories highlight the diverse and profound impact of compulsive behaviors on individuals' lives. They also underscore the importance of seeking help and support in managing and overcoming these challenges. While each journey is unique, the common thread is the resilience and determination of those who face these behaviors head-on, working towards a healthier and more fulfilling life.

Conclusion

Compulsive behaviors are complex and multifaceted, affecting individuals in various ways. From OCD and addictions to compulsive eating and hoarding, the range of behaviors is vast, each with its own set of challenges and consequences. The impact on daily life can be significant, disrupting mental and physical health, financial stability, relationships, and overall quality of life.

Personal stories and anecdotes provide valuable insights into the struggles and triumphs of those living with compulsive behaviors. They serve as a reminder that, despite the difficulties, recovery and improvement are possible with the right support and resources.

Understanding compulsive behaviors is the first step towards addressing them. By recognizing the signs, seeking professional help, and implementing effective strategies, individuals can take control of their behaviors and work towards a healthier, more balanced life.

Chapter 2: The Science Behind Compulsions

Neurological and Psychological Foundations of Compulsive Behaviors

Compulsive behaviors are deeply rooted in the complex interplay between neurological and psychological factors. Understanding these foundations is crucial to unraveling the mechanisms behind these behaviors and developing effective treatment strategies.

Neurological Foundations

1. BRAIN STRUCTURE and Function

- The Role of the Basal Ganglia: The basal ganglia, a group of nuclei located deep within the brain, are integral to the development of compulsive behaviors. These structures are involved in a variety of functions, including motor control, procedural learning, and habit formation. Abnormalities in the basal ganglia can lead to the repetitive, ritualistic actions characteristic of compulsive behaviors.

- The Orbitofrontal Cortex (OFC): The OFC, located in the frontal lobes, is crucial for decision-making and evaluating the consequences of actions. Dysfunction in the OFC can impair an individual's ability to assess the risks and benefits of their behavior, leading to compulsive actions that persist despite negative outcomes.

- The Anterior Cingulate Cortex (ACC): The ACC plays a key role in error detection, emotional regulation, and cognitive control. Hyperactivity in this region is often observed in individuals with obsessive-compulsive disorder (OCD), contributing to the heightened anxiety and compulsive checking behaviors.

2. Neurotransmitters and Compulsive Behaviors

- Serotonin: Serotonin is a neurotransmitter involved in mood regulation, impulse control, and anxiety. Low levels of serotonin have been linked to OCD and other compulsive behaviors. Selective serotonin reuptake inhibitors (SSRIs), which increase serotonin levels in the brain, are commonly used to treat these conditions.

- Dopamine: Dopamine is another critical neurotransmitter associated with the brain's reward system and the reinforcement of behaviors. Dysregulation of dopamine pathways can lead to compulsive behaviors, as individuals repeatedly engage in actions that trigger dopamine release, seeking the associated pleasure or relief.

- Glutamate: Glutamate is the primary excitatory neurotransmitter in the brain and is involved in synaptic plasticity and learning. Abnormal glutamate signaling has been implicated in OCD and other compulsive behaviors, influencing the development and persistence of these actions.

Psychological Foundations

1. COGNITIVE PROCESSES

- Intrusive Thoughts and Obsessions: Intrusive thoughts are unwanted, distressing thoughts that repeatedly enter an individual's mind. These thoughts can trigger anxiety and lead to compulsive behaviors as a means of alleviating the discomfort. In OCD, for example, obsessions about contamination or harm drive compulsive cleaning or checking behaviors.

- Maladaptive Beliefs: Individuals with compulsive behaviors often hold maladaptive beliefs that reinforce their actions. For instance, someone with OCD may believe that failing to perform a ritual will result in catastrophic consequences, perpetuating the compulsive behavior despite its irrational nature.

2. Behavioral Processes

- Negative Reinforcement: Compulsive behaviors are often maintained through negative reinforcement, where the behavior reduces or eliminates an aversive stimulus. For example, someone with compulsive handwashing may wash their hands to relieve anxiety about germs, reinforcing the behavior despite its negative impact on their life.

- Avoidance: Avoidance behaviors are common in individuals with compulsions, as they seek to avoid situations that trigger their anxiety or distress. This avoidance can perpetuate the cycle of compulsive behavior, as it prevents the individual from confronting and overcoming their fears.

The Role of Genetics and Environment

COMPULSIVE BEHAVIORS arise from a complex interplay between genetic predispositions and environmental influences. Understanding these factors can provide insight into why certain individuals develop compulsive behaviors while others do not.

Genetic Factors

1. FAMILY STUDIES

- Heritability of Compulsive Behaviors: Family studies have shown that compulsive behaviors, particularly OCD, tend to run in families. First-degree relatives of individuals with OCD are at a higher risk of developing the disorder, suggesting a genetic component. Twin studies further support this, with higher concordance rates for OCD in monozygotic (identical) twins compared to dizygotic (fraternal) twins.

2. Genetic Variants

- Candidate Genes: Research has identified several candidate genes associated with compulsive behaviors. These genes are involved in neurotransmitter systems, such as serotonin and dopamine, as well as neural development and synaptic function. For example, variations in the serotonin transporter gene (SLC6A4) and the dopamine D2 receptor gene (DRD2) have been linked to an increased risk of OCD.

- Genome-Wide Association Studies (GWAS): GWAS have identified additional genetic loci associated with compulsive behaviors. These studies scan the entire genome to find genetic variations that occur more frequently in individuals with the disorder compared to those without. While GWAS have provided valuable insights, the genetic architecture of compulsive behaviors is complex, involving multiple genes with small effects.

Environmental Factors

1. EARLY LIFE EXPERIENCES

- Trauma and Stress: Traumatic or stressful experiences in childhood, such as abuse, neglect, or significant life changes, can contribute to the development of compulsive behaviors. These experiences can lead to alterations in brain function and stress response systems, increasing vulnerability to compulsive behaviors later in life.

- Parenting Styles: Overprotective or controlling parenting styles have been associated with a higher risk of developing OCD. These parenting behaviors can create an environment of heightened anxiety and reinforce the need for control and predictability, which are common features of compulsive behaviors.

2. Social and Cultural Influences

- Cultural Norms and Expectations: Cultural norms and societal expectations can shape the expression of compulsive behaviors. For example, in cultures where cleanliness and order are highly valued, individuals may be more likely to develop compulsive cleaning behaviors. Additionally, cultural attitudes towards mental health can influence whether individuals seek help or hide their symptoms.

- Peer Influence: Social interactions and peer relationships can impact the development and maintenance of compulsive behaviors. Peer pressure, bullying, or social rejection can contribute to anxiety and stress, potentially triggering compulsive behaviors as a coping mechanism.

3. Life Events

- Significant Life Changes: Major life events, such as moving, starting a new job, or the loss of a loved one, can act as stressors that trigger or exacerbate compulsive behaviors. The disruption and uncertainty associated with these events can increase anxiety and lead individuals to seek comfort in repetitive actions.

- Chronic Stress: Ongoing stressors, such as financial difficulties, relationship problems, or health issues, can also contribute to the persistence of compulsive behaviors. Chronic stress can dysregulate the body's stress response systems and increase vulnerability to mental health disorders, including those involving compulsive behaviors.

Understanding the Brain's Reward System and How It Relates to Compulsions

THE BRAIN'S REWARD system plays a crucial role in the development and maintenance of compulsive behaviors. This system, which involves several interconnected brain regions and neurotransmitter pathways, is responsible for reinforcing behaviors that are perceived as rewarding or pleasurable. Understanding how the reward system functions and its relation to compulsive behaviors can shed light on why these behaviors are so difficult to control.

Key Components of the Brain's Reward System

1. THE MESOLIMBIC PATHWAY

- Structure and Function: The mesolimbic pathway is a key component of the brain's reward system. It connects the ventral tegmental area (VTA) in the midbrain to the nucleus accumbens in the basal ganglia. This pathway is involved in the processing of rewards, motivation, and reinforcement of behaviors.

- Dopamine Release: When an individual engages in a behavior that is perceived as rewarding, the VTA releases dopamine into the nucleus accumbens. This release of dopamine creates a sense of pleasure or satisfaction, reinforcing the behavior and increasing the likelihood of its repetition.

2. The Prefrontal Cortex

- Role in Decision-Making: The prefrontal cortex is involved in higher-order cognitive functions, including decision-making, impulse control, and evaluating the consequences of actions. It helps regulate the reward system by modulating responses to rewarding stimuli and integrating information about long-term goals and potential risks.

- Dysregulation in Compulsive Behaviors: In individuals with compulsive behaviors, the prefrontal cortex may be less effective in regulating the reward system. This dysregulation can lead to impaired decision-making and difficulty resisting urges to engage in compulsive actions, despite awareness of negative consequences.

The Role of Dopamine in Reinforcement

1. DOPAMINE AND PLEASURE

- Pleasure and Reward: Dopamine is often referred to as the "pleasure neurotransmitter" because of its role in creating feelings of pleasure and reward. When dopamine is released in response to a rewarding stimulus, it signals to the brain that the behavior is beneficial and worth repeating.

- Reinforcement of Compulsive Behaviors: In the context of compulsive behaviors, the release of dopamine reinforces the actions that led to the reward. For example, in gambling addiction, the anticipation and experience of winning trigger dopamine release, reinforcing the compulsion to continue gambling despite losses.

2. Dopamine and Learning

- Learning and Memory: Dopamine is also involved in learning and memory processes. It helps the brain associate specific behaviors with rewarding outcomes, strengthening neural pathways that support the repetition of those behaviors.

- Compulsive Learning: In compulsive behaviors, this learning process becomes maladaptive. The brain learns to associate the compulsive behavior with relief from anxiety or other negative emotions, reinforcing the behavior even when it becomes harmful.

The Role of the Reward System in Different Compulsive Behaviors

1. OCD AND THE REWARD System

- Reinforcement of Rituals: In OCD, compulsive rituals are often performed to alleviate anxiety caused by intrusive thoughts. The temporary relief provided by these rituals reinforces the behavior, making it more likely to be repeated in response to similar thoughts in the future.

- Hyperactivity in Reward Circuits: Neuroimaging studies have shown hyperactivity in reward-related brain regions, such as the nucleus accumbens, in individuals with OCD. This hyperactivity may contribute to the persistent and reinforcing nature of compulsive rituals.

2. Addictions and the Reward System

- Substance Abuse: In substance abuse disorders, drugs or alcohol directly stimulate the release of dopamine in the brain's reward pathways, creating intense feelings of pleasure. The powerful reinforcement provided by these substances leads to repeated use and eventual addiction.

- Behavioral Addictions: Behavioral addictions, such as gambling or internet addiction, also involve the reward system. Engaging in these behaviors triggers dopamine release, reinforcing the compulsion to continue the behavior despite negative consequences.

3. Compulsive Eating and the Reward System

- Food and Dopamine: Eating, especially highly palatable foods rich in sugar and fat, triggers the release of dopamine in the brain's reward pathways. This release reinforces the behavior, leading to overeating and, in some cases, compulsive eating.

- Cravings and Binge Eating: In individuals with compulsive eating behaviors, the anticipation of eating and the act of consuming food can create strong cravings and reinforce binge-eating episodes. The temporary pleasure derived from eating perpetuates the cycle of compulsive eating.

4. Compulsive Shopping and the Reward System

- Shopping and Dopamine: The act of shopping and making purchases can trigger dopamine release, creating feelings of pleasure and excitement. This reinforcement can lead to compulsive shopping behaviors, where individuals repeatedly seek the rewarding experience of buying new items.

- Financial Consequences: Despite the negative financial consequences, the immediate pleasure derived from shopping reinforces the behavior, making it difficult for individuals to control their spending.

Addressing Dysregulation in the Reward System

1. THERAPEUTIC INTERVENTIONS

- Cognitive-Behavioral Therapy (CBT): CBT is a widely used therapeutic approach for addressing compulsive behaviors. It helps individuals identify and challenge maladaptive thoughts and beliefs, develop alternative coping strategies, and reduce reliance on compulsive behaviors for relief.

- Exposure and Response Prevention (ERP): ERP is a specific form of CBT used to treat OCD. It involves gradually exposing individuals to anxiety-provoking stimuli while preventing the performance of compulsive rituals. Over time, this reduces the anxiety associated with the stimuli and weakens the reinforcement of the compulsive behavior.

2. Pharmacological Treatments

- SSRIs and Antidepressants: Medications that increase serotonin levels, such as SSRIs, are commonly prescribed for OCD and other compulsive behaviors. These medications can help reduce the intensity of obsessions and compulsions by modulating neurotransmitter activity.

- Dopamine Modulators: In cases where dopamine dysregulation plays a significant role, medications that modulate dopamine activity may be used. These can help reduce the reinforcement of compulsive behaviors by altering the brain's reward pathways.

3. Neurosurgical and Neuromodulation Techniques

- Deep Brain Stimulation (DBS): DBS is a neurosurgical technique used in severe cases of OCD that do not respond to conventional treatments. It involves implanting electrodes in specific brain regions to modulate abnormal neural activity and reduce compulsive behaviors.

- Transcranial Magnetic Stimulation (TMS): TMS is a non-invasive neuromodulation technique that uses magnetic fields to stimulate specific brain areas. It has shown promise in reducing symptoms of OCD and other compulsive behaviors by modulating neural activity in the reward system and related regions.

4. Lifestyle and Behavioral Strategies

- Mindfulness and Stress Reduction: Mindfulness practices, such as meditation and deep breathing exercises, can help individuals manage stress and anxiety, reducing the reliance on compulsive behaviors for relief.

- Healthy Habits and Routine: Establishing healthy routines and habits can provide structure and reduce the likelihood of engaging in compulsive behaviors. Regular exercise, balanced nutrition, and sufficient sleep contribute to overall well-being and resilience.

Conclusion

The science behind compulsive behaviors reveals a complex interplay of neurological, psychological, genetic, and environmental factors. The brain's reward system, with its intricate network of pathways and neurotransmitters, plays a crucial role in reinforcing these behaviors. Understanding the underlying mechanisms of compulsions is essential for developing effective treatment strategies and supporting individuals in their journey towards recovery.

By exploring the neurological and psychological foundations, the influence of genetics and environment, and the role of the brain's reward system, we gain valuable insights into the nature of compulsive behaviors. This knowledge empowers individuals, families, and healthcare professionals to address these challenges with empathy, evidence-based interventions, and a comprehensive approach to healing and recovery.

Chapter 3: Identifying Compulsive Behaviors

Signs and Symptoms of Compulsive Behaviors

Identifying compulsive behaviors early is crucial for effective intervention and treatment. Compulsive behaviors manifest in various forms and intensities, affecting different aspects of an individual's life. Recognizing the signs and symptoms can help in distinguishing these behaviors from normal habits or occasional indulgences. Here, we will explore the common signs and symptoms of compulsive behaviors, providing a comprehensive guide for identifying them.

1. Persistent and Uncontrollable Urges

- Inability to Resist: One of the hallmark signs of compulsive behavior is the persistent and overwhelming urge to perform a specific action or engage in a particular activity. Despite recognizing the behavior as irrational or harmful, individuals find it difficult to resist these urges.

- Intrusive Thoughts: These urges are often accompanied by intrusive thoughts or obsessions that dominate the individual's mind, leading to anxiety and distress.

2. Repetitive Actions

- Ritualistic Behavior: Compulsive behaviors are characterized by repetitive actions that are performed in a ritualistic manner. These actions are often aimed at reducing anxiety or preventing a perceived negative outcome.

- Frequency and Duration: The frequency and duration of these actions are excessive and disproportionate to the situation. For instance, compulsive handwashing may involve washing hands multiple times in a row for extended periods.

3. Impact on Daily Life

- Interference with Daily Activities: Compulsive behaviors can significantly interfere with an individual's daily activities, responsibilities, and routines. The time and energy spent on these behaviors can detract from work, school, or personal relationships.

- Avoidance: Individuals may go to great lengths to avoid situations that trigger their compulsive behaviors, leading to social isolation or avoidance of certain tasks or places.

4. Emotional Distress

- Anxiety and Guilt: Compulsive behaviors are often driven by anxiety and are followed by feelings of guilt or shame. The temporary relief provided by the behavior is quickly overshadowed by negative emotions.

- Depression: The ongoing struggle with compulsive behaviors and the associated emotional distress can lead to depression and a sense of hopelessness.

5. Physical Symptoms

- Fatigue and Stress: The physical toll of compulsive behaviors, such as lack of sleep, chronic stress, and fatigue, can further impact an individual's health and well-being.

- Injuries: Some compulsive behaviors, such as skin picking or hair pulling, can result in physical injuries, infections, or long-term damage to the body.

Self-Assessment Tools and Techniques

SELF-ASSESSMENT TOOLS and techniques are invaluable for individuals who suspect they may have compulsive behaviors. These tools help in identifying the presence and severity of compulsions, guiding individuals towards seeking appropriate help and treatment. Here are some effective self-assessment tools and techniques:

1. Questionnaires and Inventories

- Yale-Brown Obsessive Compulsive Scale (Y-BOCS): The Y-BOCS is a widely used tool for assessing the severity of OCD symptoms. It includes questions about the time spent on obsessions and compulsions, the level of distress they cause, and their impact on daily functioning.

- Obsessive-Compulsive Inventory (OCI): The OCI is another self-report measure that assesses the presence and severity of OCD symptoms. It covers various dimensions of OCD, including washing, checking, hoarding, and neutralizing behaviors.

2. Journaling and Monitoring

- Behavioral Logs: Keeping a daily log of behaviors can help individuals track the frequency, duration, and triggers of their compulsive actions. This information can be valuable for identifying patterns and understanding the underlying causes of the behaviors.

- Mood and Thought Records: Recording thoughts and emotions associated with compulsive behaviors can provide insight into the cognitive and emotional processes driving the actions. This technique can also help in identifying negative thought patterns and beliefs that reinforce the behaviors.

3. Behavioral Experiments

- Exposure Exercises: Behavioral experiments involve gradually exposing oneself to anxiety-provoking situations without engaging in the compulsive behavior. This technique helps in understanding the relationship between anxiety and compulsive actions and can be a step towards reducing reliance on these behaviors.

- Response Prevention: Paired with exposure exercises, response prevention involves resisting the urge to perform the compulsive behavior. Over time, this can reduce the anxiety associated with the trigger and weaken the compulsion.

4. Mindfulness and Self-Reflection

- Mindfulness Practices: Mindfulness techniques, such as meditation and deep breathing exercises, can help individuals become more aware of their thoughts and behaviors. This heightened awareness can aid in recognizing compulsive patterns and developing strategies to manage them.

- Self-Reflection: Regular self-reflection through techniques like journaling or mindfulness can provide deeper insights into the motivations and emotions behind compulsive behaviors, facilitating personal growth and change.

5. Professional Consultation

- Therapist Assessment: Consulting with a mental health professional can provide a comprehensive assessment of compulsive behaviors. Therapists can use standardized tools and clinical interviews to diagnose the condition and recommend appropriate treatments.

- Psychoeducation: Learning about compulsive behaviors from credible sources, such as books, articles, or professional workshops, can enhance understanding and provide guidance on managing the condition.

Differentiating Between Habits, Addictions, and Compulsions

UNDERSTANDING THE DISTINCTIONS between habits, addictions, and compulsions is essential for accurately identifying and addressing these behaviors. While these terms are often used interchangeably, they refer to different phenomena with unique characteristics and implications.

1. Habits

- Definition: Habits are behaviors that are performed regularly and automatically, often without conscious thought. They develop through repetition and can be positive, neutral, or negative.

- Formation: Habits form through a process of reinforcement, where a behavior is repeated in response to a specific cue and followed by a reward. Over time, this behavior becomes automatic.

- Examples: Brushing teeth before bed, checking the phone upon waking, or biting nails when nervous.

2. Addictions

- Definition: Addictions involve a compulsive need to engage in a particular activity or consume a substance, despite harmful consequences. Addictions are characterized by physical or psychological dependence.

- Characteristics: Addictions involve a cycle of craving, consumption, and withdrawal. The individual experiences intense urges to engage in the addictive behavior and may develop tolerance, requiring more of the substance or activity to achieve the same effect.

- Examples: Substance abuse (alcohol, drugs), gambling addiction, and internet addiction.

3. Compulsions

- Definition: Compulsions are repetitive behaviors or mental acts that an individual feels driven to perform in response to an obsession or according to rigid rules. The behaviors are aimed at preventing or reducing distress or preventing a feared event, but they are not connected in a realistic way to what they are designed to prevent.

- Characteristics: Compulsions are often performed to alleviate anxiety or discomfort caused by intrusive thoughts or obsessions. Unlike habits, compulsions are not typically enjoyable and are performed to achieve a temporary sense of relief.

- Examples: Compulsive handwashing, checking locks repeatedly, and counting rituals.

Key Differences

1. MOTIVATION AND PURPOSE

- Habits: Driven by routine and often performed without conscious awareness. Habits can be functional and adaptive, such as brushing teeth or exercising regularly.

- Addictions: Driven by a craving or need for a substance or activity. Addictions provide a sense of pleasure or escape, despite negative consequences.

- Compulsions: Driven by the need to reduce anxiety or prevent a perceived negative event. Compulsions provide temporary relief but are often accompanied by distress or guilt.

2. Level of Control

- Habits: Generally, individuals have more control over habits and can modify or change them with intention and effort.

- Addictions: Addictions involve a loss of control, where the individual feels compelled to engage in the behavior despite knowing its harmful effects.

- Compulsions: Compulsions also involve a loss of control, where the behavior is performed to alleviate distress but is recognized as irrational or excessive.

3. Impact on Life

- Habits: Habits can be beneficial or neutral, with minimal impact on an individual's overall functioning. Negative habits can be changed with conscious effort.

- Addictions: Addictions have a significant impact on an individual's health, relationships, and daily functioning. They often require professional intervention and support for recovery.

- Compulsions: Compulsions can severely interfere with an individual's daily life and responsibilities. They often cause significant emotional distress and may require therapeutic intervention.

Signs and Symptoms of Specific Compulsive Behaviors

TO FURTHER ILLUSTRATE the signs and symptoms of compulsive behaviors, we will explore some specific types, providing detailed descriptions and examples.

1. Obsessive-Compulsive Disorder (OCD)

- Signs and Symptoms: Intrusive thoughts or obsessions that cause significant anxiety, leading to repetitive behaviors or compulsions aimed at reducing the anxiety. Common compulsions include excessive cleaning, checking, counting, and arranging objects.

- Example: A person with OCD may spend hours each day checking that all appliances are turned off to prevent a fire, despite knowing they have already checked multiple times.

2. Compulsive Hoarding

- Signs and Symptoms: Difficulty discarding items, regardless of their value, leading to excessive accumulation and clutter. The individual may feel distress at the thought of discarding items and often believes they will need the items in the future.

- Example: A person with compulsive hoarding may fill their home with newspapers, clothing, and other items to the point that living spaces become unusable.

3. Trichotillomania (Hair-Pulling Disorder)

- Signs and Symptoms: Recurrent pulling out of one's hair, resulting in noticeable hair loss. The behavior is often preceded by an increasing sense of tension and followed by relief or gratification.

- Example: A person with trichotillomania may pull out hair from their scalp, eyebrows, or eyelashes, leading to bald patches and significant distress.

4. Dermatillomania (Skin-Picking Disorder)

- Signs and Symptoms: Recurrent skin picking, leading to skin lesions, infections, and scarring. The behavior is often a response to perceived imperfections or as a means of coping with stress or anxiety.

- Example: A person with dermatillomania may spend hours each day picking at their skin, causing open sores and significant physical damage.

5. Compulsive Eating (Binge Eating Disorder)

- Signs and Symptoms: Episodes of eating large quantities of food in a short period, often accompanied by a sense of loss of control. These episodes are followed by feelings of guilt, shame, and distress.

- Example: A person with compulsive eating may consume large amounts of food in secret and feel unable to stop eating despite feeling full.

6. Compulsive Shopping (Oniomania)

- Signs and Symptoms: An uncontrollable urge to shop and make purchases, leading to financial problems and distress. The behavior is often driven by the need to alleviate negative emotions or achieve a temporary sense of gratification.

- Example: A person with compulsive shopping may buy unnecessary items and hide purchases from family members, accumulating significant debt.

Self-Assessment Techniques in Detail

LET'S DELVE DEEPER into some of the self-assessment techniques and how they can be applied to identify and understand compulsive behaviors.

1. Questionnaires and Inventories

Yale-Brown Obsessive Compulsive Scale (Y-BOCS)

- PURPOSE: THE Y-BOCS is designed to assess the severity of obsessive-compulsive symptoms in individuals.

- Structure: It consists of a symptom checklist and a severity scale, covering various dimensions of OCD symptoms.

- Scoring: The severity scale includes questions about the time spent on obsessions and compulsions, the level of distress caused, and their impact on daily functioning. Scores range from mild to severe, guiding the need for intervention.

- Application: Individuals can complete the Y-BOCS with the help of a therapist or as a self-assessment tool. The results can provide valuable insights into the severity of symptoms and inform treatment decisions.

Obsessive-Compulsive Inventory (OCI)

- PURPOSE: THE OCI IS another self-report measure that assesses the presence and severity of OCD symptoms.

- Structure: It includes questions about different types of compulsions, such as washing, checking, hoarding, and mental rituals.

- Scoring: The inventory provides a total score and subscale scores for different symptom dimensions, helping to identify specific areas of concern.

- Application: The OCI can be used as part of a comprehensive assessment by mental health professionals or as a self-assessment tool for individuals seeking to understand their symptoms.

2. Journaling and Monitoring

Behavioral Logs

- PURPOSE: KEEPING A behavioral log helps individuals track the frequency, duration, and triggers of their compulsive behaviors.

- Structure: The log can include columns for the date, time, behavior, duration, trigger, and associated thoughts and emotions.

- Benefits: By maintaining a log, individuals can identify patterns and trends in their behaviors, providing valuable information for self-reflection and therapy.

Mood and Thought Records

- PURPOSE: RECORDING thoughts and emotions associated with compulsive behaviors helps individuals understand the cognitive and emotional processes driving their actions.

- Structure: A mood and thought record can include columns for the date, situation, thoughts, emotions, behavior, and alternative responses.

- Benefits: This technique promotes self-awareness and helps individuals identify and challenge negative thought patterns that reinforce compulsive behaviors.

3. Behavioral Experiments

Exposure Exercises

- PURPOSE: EXPOSURE exercises involve gradually exposing oneself to anxiety-provoking situations without engaging in the compulsive behavior.

- Structure: The exercises can be structured hierarchically, starting with less anxiety-provoking situations and gradually progressing to more challenging ones.

- Benefits: Exposure exercises help individuals confront their fears and reduce reliance on compulsive behaviors for relief. Over time, this can lead to a decrease in anxiety and compulsions.

Response Prevention

- PURPOSE: RESPONSE prevention involves resisting the urge to perform the compulsive behavior.

- Structure: This technique is often used in conjunction with exposure exercises, where individuals are exposed to triggers but prevented from engaging in the compulsive action.

- Benefits: Response prevention helps individuals break the cycle of compulsion and reduces the reinforcement of the behavior. It can be challenging but is effective in the long term.

4. Mindfulness and Self-Reflection

Mindfulness Practices

- PURPOSE: MINDFULNESS techniques help individuals become more aware of their thoughts and behaviors in the present moment.

- Structure: Practices can include meditation, deep breathing exercises, and body scans.

- Benefits: Mindfulness enhances self-awareness and can help individuals recognize compulsive patterns and develop strategies to manage them.

Self-Reflection

- PURPOSE: REGULAR SELF-reflection helps individuals gain deeper insights into the motivations and emotions behind their compulsive behaviors.

- Structure: Techniques can include journaling, mindfulness meditation, and reflective exercises guided by a therapist.

- Benefits: Self-reflection promotes personal growth and change by fostering a deeper understanding of oneself and one's behaviors.

5. Professional Consultation

Therapist Assessment

- PURPOSE: CONSULTING with a mental health professional provides a comprehensive assessment of compulsive behaviors.

- Structure: Therapists use standardized tools, clinical interviews, and diagnostic criteria to assess the presence and severity of compulsive behaviors.

- Benefits: Professional consultation ensures accurate diagnosis and personalized treatment recommendations, providing a clear path towards recovery.

Psychoeducation

- Purpose: Learning about compulsive behaviors from credible sources enhances understanding and provides guidance on managing the condition.

- Structure: Psychoeducation can include reading books, attending workshops, and participating in support groups.

- Benefits: Knowledge empowers individuals to make informed decisions about their treatment and self-management strategies.

Conclusion

Identifying compulsive behaviors involves recognizing the signs and symptoms, utilizing self-assessment tools and techniques, and understanding the distinctions between habits, addictions, and compulsions. By gaining a comprehensive understanding of these behaviors, individuals can take proactive steps towards seeking help and managing their condition.

Self-assessment tools, such as questionnaires, journaling, and behavioral experiments, provide valuable insights into the nature and severity of compulsive behaviors. Mindfulness and self-reflection techniques further enhance self-awareness and promote personal growth. Professional consultation ensures accurate diagnosis and tailored treatment plans, guiding individuals on their journey towards recovery.

Ultimately, understanding and identifying compulsive behaviors is the first step towards effective intervention and improved quality of life. With the right tools, techniques, and support, individuals can overcome the challenges posed by compulsive behaviors and work towards a healthier, more balanced future.

Chapter 4: The Emotional Toll of Compulsive Behaviors

Emotional and Mental Health Consequences

Compulsive behaviors can have a profound impact on an individual's emotional and mental health. These behaviors, which are often driven by underlying anxiety or distress, can perpetuate a cycle of negative emotions, leading to significant psychological consequences.

1. Anxiety and Stress

- Persistent Anxiety: Compulsive behaviors are frequently driven by intense anxiety. For example, individuals with OCD may perform compulsive rituals to alleviate the anxiety caused by intrusive thoughts. However, these rituals often only provide temporary relief, leading to a persistent state of heightened anxiety.

- Chronic Stress: The ongoing need to perform compulsive behaviors can create a constant state of stress. The individual may feel trapped in a cycle of anxiety and compulsion, unable to find lasting relief.

2. Depression

- Feelings of Hopelessness: The persistent nature of compulsive behaviors and the inability to control them can lead to feelings of hopelessness and despair. The individual may feel that they will never be able to overcome their compulsions, leading to a sense of futility.

- Loss of Interest and Pleasure: Depression often accompanies compulsive behaviors, with individuals losing interest in activities they once enjoyed. The time and energy spent on compulsions can detract from engaging in pleasurable or meaningful activities.

3. Guilt and Shame

- Self-Blame: Individuals with compulsive behaviors often blame themselves for their inability to control their actions. This self-blame can lead to feelings of guilt and shame, further exacerbating the emotional toll.

- Social Stigma: The societal stigma associated with compulsive behaviors can intensify feelings of shame. Individuals may fear judgment or rejection from others, leading them to hide their behaviors and avoid seeking help.

4. Low Self-Esteem

- Negative Self-Perception: The struggle with compulsive behaviors can significantly impact an individual's self-esteem. They may view themselves as weak or flawed, leading to a negative self-image.

- Impaired Functioning: The interference of compulsive behaviors in daily life can contribute to feelings of inadequacy. The individual may struggle with work, school, or personal responsibilities, leading to a diminished sense of self-worth.

5. Emotional Exhaustion

- Constant Vigilance: Managing compulsive behaviors requires constant vigilance and effort. The individual may feel emotionally exhausted from the ongoing battle with their compulsions.

- Burnout: The emotional and mental strain of compulsive behaviors can lead to burnout, where the individual feels overwhelmed and unable to cope with their daily responsibilities.

How Compulsive Behaviors Affect Relationships and Social Interactions

THE IMPACT OF COMPULSIVE behaviors extends beyond the individual, affecting their relationships and social interactions. The emotional toll of these behaviors can strain personal connections and create challenges in maintaining healthy and supportive relationships.

1. Strained Relationships

- Family Dynamics: Compulsive behaviors can significantly affect family dynamics. Family members may struggle to understand the nature of the behaviors and the underlying distress driving them. This lack of understanding can lead to frustration, resentment, and conflict.

- Partner Relationships: Romantic relationships can also be affected by compulsive behaviors. The partner may feel neglected or burdened by the individual's compulsions, leading to tension and potential breakdown of the relationship.

2. Social Isolation

- Avoidance of Social Situations: Individuals with compulsive behaviors may avoid social situations due to fear of judgment or embarrassment. They may isolate themselves to prevent others from witnessing their behaviors, leading to social withdrawal.

- Loneliness: The isolation resulting from compulsive behaviors can lead to feelings of loneliness and social disconnection. The individual may feel misunderstood and unsupported, exacerbating their emotional distress.

3. Impact on Friendships

- Reduced Social Engagement: Compulsive behaviors can reduce an individual's ability to engage in social activities. They may cancel plans or avoid outings due to their need to perform compulsive actions or manage their anxiety.

- Erosion of Trust: Friends may struggle to understand the compulsive behaviors and may feel hurt or confused by the individual's actions. This lack of understanding can erode trust and weaken the friendship.

4. Work and School Relationships

- Professional Challenges: Compulsive behaviors can interfere with job performance and relationships with colleagues. The individual may struggle to meet work demands or deadlines, leading to tension with supervisors and coworkers.

- Academic Impact: For students, compulsive behaviors can hinder academic performance and relationships with peers and teachers. The time and energy spent on managing compulsions can detract from academic responsibilities and social interactions.

The Cycle of Shame and Guilt

THE CYCLE OF SHAME and guilt is a common and pervasive aspect of compulsive behaviors. This cycle can intensify the emotional toll and create barriers to seeking help and recovery.

1. The Onset of Shame and Guilt

- Recognition of Behavior: Individuals with compulsive behaviors are often aware that their actions are irrational or excessive. This awareness can lead to feelings of shame, as they recognize the behavior is not in line with societal norms or their own values.

- Internalized Stigma: The societal stigma associated with mental health disorders and compulsive behaviors can be internalized, leading individuals to feel ashamed of their condition. They may view their behavior as a personal failing rather than a symptom of a disorder.

2. Avoidance and Concealment

- Hiding Behaviors: To avoid judgment or rejection, individuals may go to great lengths to hide their compulsive behaviors from others. This concealment can create additional stress and anxiety, as they fear being discovered.

- Avoidance of Help: Shame and guilt can prevent individuals from seeking help. They may fear that admitting to their compulsive behaviors will lead to further judgment or confirmation of their perceived inadequacy.

3. Perpetuation of Compulsive Behaviors

- Negative Reinforcement: The temporary relief provided by compulsive behaviors can reinforce the cycle. The individual may continue to engage in the behavior to alleviate anxiety, despite the subsequent feelings of shame and guilt.

- Increased Isolation: The shame and guilt associated with compulsive behaviors can lead to increased isolation and withdrawal from social interactions. This isolation can further perpetuate the behaviors, as the individual lacks support and understanding.

4. Impact on Self-Esteem

- Negative Self-Image: The ongoing cycle of shame and guilt can erode an individual's self-esteem. They may view themselves as inherently flawed or unworthy, leading to a negative self-image.

- Self-Criticism: Individuals may engage in self-criticism and negative self-talk, reinforcing feelings of inadequacy and hopelessness.

5. Breaking the Cycle

- Acknowledgment and Acceptance: Breaking the cycle of shame and guilt begins with acknowledging and accepting the compulsive behaviors as symptoms of a disorder. This acceptance can reduce self-blame and create a foundation for seeking help.

- Seeking Support: Reaching out for support from friends, family, or mental health professionals can provide validation and understanding. Supportive relationships can help individuals feel less alone and more empowered to address their behaviors.

- Therapeutic Interventions: Therapy, such as cognitive-behavioral therapy (CBT) or acceptance and commitment therapy (ACT), can help individuals challenge negative thought patterns and develop healthier coping strategies. These interventions can reduce the emotional toll and facilitate recovery.

Detailed Exploration of the Emotional Toll

Anxiety and Stress in Depth

ANXIETY AND STRESS are central to the experience of compulsive behaviors. Understanding the mechanisms and manifestations of these emotions can provide insight into the challenges faced by individuals with compulsions.

1. Mechanisms of Anxiety

- Fight-or-Flight Response: Anxiety triggers the body's fight-or-flight response, leading to physiological changes such as increased heart rate, rapid breathing, and heightened alertness. This response is intended to prepare the body to face or escape perceived threats.

- Cognitive Processes: Anxiety involves cognitive processes that amplify perceived threats and risks. Individuals may engage in catastrophic thinking, where they anticipate the worst possible outcomes.

2. Manifestations of Anxiety

- Physical Symptoms: Anxiety can manifest in physical symptoms such as headaches, muscle tension, gastrointestinal issues, and fatigue. These symptoms can further impact an individual's quality of life and well-being.

- Behavioral Symptoms: Anxiety can lead to avoidance behaviors, where individuals avoid situations or activities that trigger their anxiety. This avoidance can reinforce the anxiety and perpetuate the cycle of compulsive behaviors.

3. Impact of Chronic Stress

- Physiological Effects: Chronic stress can have significant physiological effects, including a weakened immune system, cardiovascular issues, and increased risk of chronic illnesses.

- Emotional Effects: Ongoing stress can lead to emotional exhaustion, irritability, and difficulty concentrating. The constant state of alertness and worry can take a toll on mental health.

Depression and Compulsive Behaviors

THE RELATIONSHIP BETWEEN depression and compulsive behaviors is complex and bidirectional. Compulsive behaviors can contribute to the development of depression, and depression can exacerbate compulsive behaviors.

1. Contributing Factors to Depression

- Sense of Helplessness: The inability to control compulsive behaviors can lead to a sense of helplessness and powerlessness, which are key factors in the development of depression.

- Loss of Enjoyment: The time and energy spent on compulsive behaviors can detract from engaging in activities that bring joy and fulfillment. This loss of enjoyment can contribute to depressive symptoms.

2. Symptoms of Depression

- Emotional Symptoms: Depression is characterized by persistent sadness, hopelessness, and a lack of interest in activities. Individuals may experience feelings of worthlessness and excessive guilt.

- Physical Symptoms: Depression can also manifest in physical symptoms such as changes in appetite and sleep patterns, fatigue, and difficulty concentrating.

3. Impact on Compulsive Behaviors

- Increased Compulsions: Depression can increase the severity and frequency of compulsive behaviors. Individuals may rely more heavily on these behaviors as a means of coping with depressive symptoms.

- Reduced Motivation for Treatment: Depression can reduce motivation to seek treatment or engage in therapeutic interventions. The individual may feel that recovery is unattainable, leading to a sense of resignation.

Guilt and Shame: A Closer Look

GUILT AND SHAME ARE pervasive emotions in the experience of compulsive behaviors. Understanding the nuances of these emotions can provide insight into their impact and the strategies for addressing them.

1. Nature of Guilt and Shame

- Guilt: Guilt arises from the perception of having done something wrong or harmful. It is often related to specific actions or behaviors and can lead to feelings of remorse and regret.

- Shame: Shame is a more pervasive and internalized emotion, arising from the perception of being fundamentally flawed or inadequate. It is often related to one's self-identity and can lead to feelings of worthlessness and humiliation.

2. Sources of Guilt and Shame

- Internalized Stigma: The stigma associated with mental health disorders and compulsive behaviors can be internalized, leading individuals to feel ashamed of their condition. They may view their behaviors as a personal failing rather than a symptom of a disorder.

- Self-Blame: Individuals may blame themselves for their inability to control their compulsive behaviors. This self-blame can lead to feelings of guilt and shame, further exacerbating the emotional toll.

3. Impact on Behavior and Well-Being

- Avoidance and Concealment: To avoid judgment or rejection, individuals may go to great lengths to hide their compulsive behaviors from others. This concealment can create additional stress and anxiety, as they fear being discovered.

- Isolation and Withdrawal: The shame and guilt associated with compulsive behaviors can lead to increased isolation and withdrawal from social interactions. This isolation can further perpetuate the behaviors, as the individual lacks support and understanding.

4. Strategies for Addressing Guilt and Shame

- Self-Compassion: Developing self-compassion can help individuals reduce self-blame and treat themselves with kindness and understanding. Self-compassion involves recognizing that suffering and imperfection are part of the human experience and that one deserves care and support.

- Cognitive Restructuring: Cognitive restructuring techniques, such as those used in cognitive-behavioral therapy (CBT), can help individuals challenge and reframe negative thought patterns that contribute to guilt and shame. This process involves identifying irrational beliefs and replacing them with more balanced and realistic thoughts.

- Therapeutic Interventions: Therapy, such as acceptance and commitment therapy (ACT) or dialectical behavior therapy (DBT), can help individuals develop healthier ways of coping with guilt and shame. These therapies focus on acceptance, mindfulness, and developing adaptive strategies for managing emotions.

- Social Support: Reaching out for support from friends, family, or support groups can provide validation and understanding. Supportive relationships can help individuals feel less alone and more empowered to address their behaviors.

The Interplay of Emotions and Compulsive Behaviors

UNDERSTANDING THE INTRICATE interplay of emotions and compulsive behaviors is crucial for developing effective strategies for managing and overcoming these behaviors. This section explores the connections between different emotional states and compulsive behaviors, providing insights into how these emotions interact and influence each other.

Anxiety and Compulsive Behaviors

ANXIETY IS A CENTRAL driver of many compulsive behaviors. Understanding how anxiety influences compulsions can provide valuable insights into managing and reducing these behaviors.

1. The Role of Anxiety in Compulsive Behaviors

- Triggering Compulsions: Anxiety often triggers compulsive behaviors as a means of coping with or reducing the distress caused by intrusive thoughts or fears. For example, someone with OCD may perform rituals to alleviate anxiety about contamination or harm.

- Temporary Relief: Compulsive behaviors provide temporary relief from anxiety, reinforcing the behavior and creating a cycle of anxiety and compulsion. The relief is short-lived, leading to the need to repeat the behavior.

2. Strategies for Managing Anxiety

- Exposure and Response Prevention (ERP): ERP is a therapeutic technique that involves gradually exposing individuals to anxiety-provoking situations while preventing the performance of compulsive behaviors. This approach helps reduce the anxiety associated with the triggers and weakens the reinforcement of the compulsions.

- Relaxation Techniques: Relaxation techniques, such as deep breathing, progressive muscle relaxation, and guided imagery, can help individuals manage anxiety and reduce the urge to engage in compulsive behaviors.

- Mindfulness and Meditation: Mindfulness and meditation practices can help individuals become more aware of their thoughts and emotions, reducing the impact of anxiety and improving emotional regulation.

Depression and Compulsive Behaviors

THE RELATIONSHIP BETWEEN depression and compulsive behaviors is complex and can create a vicious cycle that is challenging to break.

1. Depression as a Consequence of Compulsive Behaviors

- Impact on Quality of Life: The interference of compulsive behaviors in daily life can lead to a reduced quality of life, contributing to feelings of hopelessness and depression.

- Social Isolation: The isolation resulting from compulsive behaviors can exacerbate depressive symptoms, leading to a sense of loneliness and disconnection.

2. Compulsive Behaviors as a Coping Mechanism

- Temporary Escape: Compulsive behaviors can provide a temporary escape from depressive symptoms, offering a brief sense of relief or distraction.

- Reinforcement of Behaviors: The temporary relief provided by compulsive behaviors reinforces the cycle, making it difficult to break free from the behaviors and address the underlying depression.

3. Strategies for Addressing Depression

- Therapy: Cognitive-behavioral therapy (CBT) and other therapeutic approaches can help individuals address depressive symptoms and develop healthier coping strategies. Therapy can also help individuals understand the relationship between their compulsive behaviors and depression.

- Medication: Antidepressant medications, such as selective serotonin reuptake inhibitors (SSRIs), can help manage depressive symptoms and reduce the severity of compulsive behaviors. Medication should be used in conjunction with therapy for optimal outcomes.

- Lifestyle Changes: Engaging in regular physical activity, maintaining a balanced diet, and establishing a consistent sleep routine can improve overall well-being and reduce depressive symptoms.

Guilt, Shame, and Compulsive Behaviors

GUILT AND SHAME ARE powerful emotions that can perpetuate compulsive behaviors and create barriers to seeking help and recovery.

1. The Impact of Guilt and Shame

- Internalized Stigma: The internalization of societal stigma associated with compulsive behaviors can lead to feelings of guilt and shame, further exacerbating the emotional toll.

- Self-Blame: Individuals may blame themselves for their compulsive behaviors, viewing them as a personal failing rather than a symptom of a disorder.

2. Addressing Guilt and Shame

- Developing Self-Compassion: Cultivating self-compassion involves treating oneself with kindness and understanding, recognizing that suffering and imperfection are part of the human experience. Self-compassion can reduce self-blame and promote emotional healing.

- Challenging Negative Thought Patterns: Cognitive restructuring techniques can help individuals identify and challenge negative thought patterns that contribute to guilt and shame. Reframing irrational beliefs can lead to a more balanced and realistic self-perception.

- Seeking Support: Reaching out for support from friends, family, or support groups can provide validation and understanding. Supportive relationships can help individuals feel less alone and more empowered to address their behaviors.

Conclusion

The emotional toll of compulsive behaviors is significant and multifaceted, impacting an individual's mental health, relationships, and overall quality of life. Understanding the emotional and psychological consequences of these behaviors is crucial for developing effective strategies for managing and overcoming them.

Compulsive behaviors are often driven by underlying anxiety and distress, leading to a cycle of temporary relief and subsequent guilt and shame. This cycle can perpetuate the behaviors and create barriers to seeking help and recovery. The impact on relationships and social interactions can further exacerbate the emotional toll, leading to isolation and increased distress.

Breaking the cycle of shame and guilt involves acknowledging and accepting compulsive behaviors as symptoms of a disorder, seeking support, and engaging in therapeutic interventions. Developing self-compassion, challenging negative thought patterns, and building supportive relationships can help individuals reduce the emotional toll and work towards recovery.

By understanding the emotional toll of compulsive behaviors and addressing the underlying emotions, individuals can take proactive steps towards improving their mental health and overall well-being. With the right tools, techniques, and support, it is possible to overcome the challenges posed by compulsive behaviors and achieve a healthier, more balanced future.

Chapter 5: Seeking Professional Help

Types of Therapy and Counseling for Compulsive Behaviors

When facing compulsive behaviors, seeking professional help is often a crucial step towards recovery. Various types of therapy and counseling have been developed to address the complexities of these behaviors, each offering unique approaches and benefits. Understanding the different therapeutic options can help individuals and their families make informed decisions about their treatment plans.

1. Cognitive-Behavioral Therapy (CBT)

- Overview: CBT is a widely used therapeutic approach that focuses on identifying and challenging negative thought patterns and behaviors. It is particularly effective for treating obsessive-compulsive disorder (OCD) and other compulsive behaviors.

- Techniques: CBT involves techniques such as cognitive restructuring, which helps individuals identify and reframe irrational beliefs, and behavioral experiments, which test the validity of these beliefs. Another key component is exposure and response prevention (ERP), where individuals are gradually exposed to anxiety-provoking situations and taught to resist the urge to perform compulsive behaviors.

- Effectiveness: Numerous studies have demonstrated the effectiveness of CBT in reducing the severity and frequency of compulsive behaviors. It helps individuals develop healthier coping strategies and improve their overall functioning.

2. Exposure and Response Prevention (ERP)

- Overview: ERP is a specific form of CBT that focuses on reducing the anxiety associated with obsessive thoughts and preventing the performance of compulsive behaviors.

- Techniques: ERP involves systematic and controlled exposure to feared stimuli or situations while preventing the compulsive response. Over time, this reduces the anxiety associated with the trigger and weakens the reinforcement of the compulsive behavior.

- Effectiveness: ERP has been shown to be highly effective for individuals with OCD. It helps them break the cycle of obsession and compulsion, leading to significant improvements in symptoms and quality of life.

3. Acceptance and Commitment Therapy (ACT)

- Overview: ACT is a therapeutic approach that emphasizes acceptance of distressing thoughts and feelings rather than attempting to eliminate them. It focuses on helping individuals commit to actions that align with their values.

- Techniques: ACT uses techniques such as mindfulness, which helps individuals become more aware of their thoughts and emotions without judgment, and values clarification, which helps them identify and pursue meaningful goals. Cognitive defusion techniques are also used to reduce the impact of distressing thoughts.

- Effectiveness: ACT has shown promise in treating a variety of compulsive behaviors. It helps individuals develop psychological flexibility and improve their ability to cope with distress.

4. Dialectical Behavior Therapy (DBT)

- Overview: DBT is a form of therapy originally developed for treating borderline personality disorder but has been adapted for other conditions, including compulsive behaviors. It combines cognitive-behavioral techniques with mindfulness practices.

- Techniques: DBT includes skills training in areas such as emotion regulation, distress tolerance, interpersonal effectiveness, and mindfulness. It also involves individual therapy and group skills training sessions.

- Effectiveness: DBT is effective in reducing self-destructive behaviors and improving emotional regulation. It helps individuals develop healthier ways of coping with distress and improve their interpersonal relationships.

5. Mindfulness-Based Cognitive Therapy (MBCT)

- Overview: MBCT combines cognitive-behavioral techniques with mindfulness practices to help individuals manage their thoughts and emotions. It is often used to prevent relapse in individuals with recurrent depression but can also be effective for compulsive behaviors.

- Techniques: MBCT involves mindfulness meditation, which helps individuals become more aware of their present-moment experiences, and cognitive-behavioral techniques, which help them challenge negative thought patterns.

- Effectiveness: MBCT has been shown to be effective in reducing the severity of compulsive behaviors and preventing relapse. It helps individuals develop a greater sense of control over their thoughts and emotions.

6. Behavioral Therapy

- Overview: Behavioral therapy focuses on changing maladaptive behaviors through techniques such as positive reinforcement, punishment, and modeling.

- Techniques: Techniques used in behavioral therapy include systematic desensitization, where individuals are gradually exposed to feared stimuli while practicing relaxation techniques, and aversion therapy, where undesirable behaviors are paired with unpleasant stimuli to reduce their occurrence.

- Effectiveness: Behavioral therapy can be effective in reducing compulsive behaviors, particularly when combined with other therapeutic approaches.

7. Psychodynamic Therapy

- Overview: Psychodynamic therapy focuses on exploring unconscious thoughts and feelings that may be contributing to compulsive behaviors. It aims to help individuals gain insight into their behavior and develop healthier ways of coping.

- Techniques: Techniques used in psychodynamic therapy include free association, where individuals are encouraged to express their thoughts and feelings without censorship, and interpretation, where the therapist helps them understand the underlying meaning of their behavior.

- Effectiveness: Psychodynamic therapy can be effective for individuals with compulsive behaviors, particularly when there are underlying emotional conflicts contributing to the behavior.

8. Family Therapy

- Overview: Family therapy involves working with the individual and their family members to address the impact of compulsive behaviors on family dynamics. It aims to improve communication, reduce conflict, and enhance support.

- Techniques: Techniques used in family therapy include systemic interventions, where the therapist helps the family identify and change patterns of interaction that may be contributing to the compulsive behaviors, and psychoeducation, where the family learns about the condition and how to support the individual.

- Effectiveness: Family therapy can be effective in improving family functioning and reducing the impact of compulsive behaviors on the family. It helps the family develop healthier ways of supporting the individual and managing the condition.

9. Group Therapy

- Overview: Group therapy involves working with a group of individuals who share similar challenges. It provides a supportive environment where individuals can share their experiences, learn from others, and develop new coping strategies.

- Techniques: Techniques used in group therapy include group discussions, role-playing, and skill-building exercises. The therapist facilitates the group and provides guidance and support.

- Effectiveness: Group therapy can be effective in reducing feelings of isolation and providing social support. It helps individuals develop a sense of community and learn from the experiences of others.

Medication Options and Their Effectiveness

IN ADDITION TO THERAPY, medication can be an important component of treatment for compulsive behaviors. Various medications have been shown to be effective in reducing the severity and frequency of these behaviors. Understanding the different medication options and their effectiveness can help individuals and their healthcare providers make informed decisions about their treatment plans.

1. Selective Serotonin Reuptake Inhibitors (SSRIs)

- Overview: SSRIs are a class of antidepressants that increase the levels of serotonin in the brain. They are commonly used to treat depression, anxiety, and OCD.

- Medications: Common SSRIs include fluoxetine (Prozac), sertraline (Zoloft), and fluvoxamine (Luvox).

- Effectiveness: SSRIs have been shown to be effective in reducing the severity of compulsive behaviors, particularly in individuals with OCD. They help alleviate anxiety and improve overall functioning.

- Side Effects: Common side effects of SSRIs include nausea, headache, insomnia, and sexual dysfunction. These side effects are usually mild and decrease over time.

2. Tricyclic Antidepressants (TCAs)

- Overview: TCAs are an older class of antidepressants that increase the levels of serotonin and norepinephrine in the brain. They are sometimes used to treat OCD and other compulsive behaviors.

- Medications: Common TCAs include clomipramine (Anafranil) and amitriptyline (Elavil).

- Effectiveness: TCAs have been shown to be effective in reducing the severity of compulsive behaviors, particularly in individuals with OCD. Clomipramine is considered one of the most effective medications for OCD.

- Side Effects: Common side effects of TCAs include dry mouth, constipation, dizziness, and weight gain. These side effects can be more pronounced than those of SSRIs.

3. Serotonin-Norepinephrine Reuptake Inhibitors (SNRIs)

- Overview: SNRIs are a class of antidepressants that increase the levels of serotonin and norepinephrine in the brain. They are used to treat depression, anxiety, and OCD.

- Medications: Common SNRIs include venlafaxine (Effexor) and duloxetine (Cymbalta).

- Effectiveness: SNRIs have been shown to be effective in reducing the severity of compulsive behaviors, particularly in individuals with OCD. They help alleviate anxiety and improve overall functioning.

- Side Effects: Common side effects of SNRIs include nausea, headache, insomnia, and sexual dysfunction. These side effects are usually mild and decrease over time.

4. Benzodiazepines

- Overview: Benzodiazepines are a class of medications that enhance the effects of the neurotransmitter gamma-aminobutyric acid (GABA). They are used to treat anxiety and panic disorders.

- Medications: Common benzodiazepines include diazepam (Valium), lorazepam (Ativan), and alprazolam (Xanax).

- Effectiveness: Benzodiazepines can be effective in reducing anxiety and providing short-term relief from compulsive behaviors. However, they are not recommended for long-term use due to the risk of dependence and tolerance.

- Side Effects: Common side effects of benzodiazepines include drowsiness, dizziness, and impaired coordination. Long-term use can lead to dependence and withdrawal symptoms.

5. Antipsychotics

- Overview: Antipsychotics are a class of medications used to treat psychotic disorders, such as schizophrenia. They are sometimes used as adjunctive treatment for OCD and other compulsive behaviors.

- Medications: Common antipsychotics include risperidone (Risperdal), aripiprazole (Abilify), and quetiapine (Seroquel).

- Effectiveness: Antipsychotics can be effective in reducing the severity of compulsive behaviors, particularly when used in combination with SSRIs or other antidepressants. They are often used when individuals do not respond to standard treatments.

- Side Effects: Common side effects of antipsychotics include weight gain, drowsiness, and metabolic changes. Long-term use can lead to movement disorders, such as tardive dyskinesia.

6. Glutamate Modulators

- Overview: Glutamate modulators are a class of medications that target the glutamate system in the brain. They are being studied as potential treatments for OCD and other compulsive behaviors.

- Medications: Common glutamate modulators include memantine (Namenda) and riluzole (Rilutek).

- Effectiveness: Preliminary research suggests that glutamate modulators may be effective in reducing the severity of compulsive behaviors. They are often used as adjunctive treatments when individuals do not respond to standard medications.

- Side Effects: Common side effects of glutamate modulators include dizziness, headache, and gastrointestinal issues. More research is needed to fully understand their safety and effectiveness.

7. Complementary and Alternative Medicines (CAM)

- Overview: CAM includes a variety of treatments, such as herbal supplements, acupuncture, and meditation, that are used to complement traditional medical treatments.

- Medications: Common CAM treatments include St. John's wort, omega-3 fatty acids, and mindfulness meditation.

- Effectiveness: The effectiveness of CAM treatments for compulsive behaviors varies. Some individuals may find them helpful in reducing symptoms and improving overall well-being. However, more research is needed to fully understand their effectiveness.

- Side Effects: The side effects of CAM treatments vary depending on the specific treatment. It is important to consult with a healthcare provider before starting any CAM treatment to ensure safety and avoid potential interactions with other medications.

Finding the Right Therapist or Support Group

FINDING THE RIGHT THERAPIST or support group is a crucial step in the journey towards recovery from compulsive behaviors. The right support can provide validation, understanding, and guidance, helping individuals develop effective strategies for managing their condition.

1. Identifying Your Needs

- Assessing Your Condition: Before seeking a therapist or support group, it is important to assess your condition and identify your specific needs. Consider the severity of your compulsive behaviors, any co-occurring conditions, and your treatment goals.

- Personal Preferences: Consider your personal preferences, such as the type of therapy you are interested in, the qualifications and experience of the therapist, and the format of the support group. These factors can help you find a provider or group that aligns with your needs and preferences.

2. Finding a Qualified Therapist

- Qualifications and Credentials: Look for a therapist who is licensed and has the appropriate qualifications and credentials. This may include a degree in psychology, counseling, or social work, as well as specialized training in treating compulsive behaviors.

- Experience and Expertise: Consider the therapist's experience and expertise in treating compulsive behaviors. Look for a provider who has experience working with individuals who have similar conditions and has a track record of success.

- Therapeutic Approach: Consider the therapist's therapeutic approach and whether it aligns with your preferences and needs. Some therapists may specialize in CBT, while others may use ACT, DBT, or other approaches.

- Personal Fit: Finding a therapist who is a good personal fit is important for building a trusting and supportive therapeutic relationship. Consider factors such as the therapist's communication style, empathy, and ability to create a safe and non-judgmental environment.

3. Finding a Support Group

- Types of Support Groups: There are various types of support groups available, including in-person groups, online groups, and groups facilitated by mental health professionals. Consider the format that best suits your needs and preferences.

- Group Focus: Look for a support group that focuses on compulsive behaviors or related conditions. Some groups may be specific to certain types of compulsive behaviors, such as OCD or hoarding, while others may be more general.

- Group Dynamics: Consider the dynamics of the group, including the size of the group, the level of participation, and the overall atmosphere. A supportive and understanding group can provide a sense of community and validation.

- Facilitator Qualifications: If the group is facilitated by a mental health professional, consider their qualifications and experience. A qualified facilitator can provide guidance, structure, and support to the group.

4. Resources for Finding Help

- Professional Associations: Professional associations, such as the American Psychological Association (APA) or the National Association of Social Workers (NASW), can provide directories of qualified therapists. These directories often include information about the therapist's qualifications, experience, and areas of expertise.

- Mental Health Organizations: Mental health organizations, such as the National Alliance on Mental Illness (NAMI) or the Anxiety and Depression Association of America (ADAA), can provide resources and referrals for finding therapists and support groups.

- Online Directories: Online directories, such as Psychology Today or GoodTherapy, can provide listings of therapists and support groups. These directories often include detailed profiles of providers, including their qualifications, therapeutic approach, and contact information.

- Referrals: Referrals from healthcare providers, friends, or family members can also be valuable in finding a qualified therapist or support group. Personal recommendations can provide insight into the provider's effectiveness and suitability.

5. Evaluating Potential Therapists and Support Groups

- Initial Consultation: Many therapists offer an initial consultation to discuss your needs and treatment goals. This consultation can help you determine if the therapist is a good fit and if their approach aligns with your preferences.

- Questions to Ask: During the initial consultation, consider asking questions such as:

- What is your experience and expertise in treating compulsive behaviors?

- What therapeutic approach do you use, and how does it work?

- What is your availability and session structure?

- How do you measure progress and success in treatment?

- Trial Period: Consider starting with a trial period to see if the therapist or support group is a good fit. It is important to feel comfortable and supported in your treatment, and it is okay to seek a different provider or group if necessary.

6. Building a Support Network

- Collaborative Care: Building a support network involves collaborating with healthcare providers, therapists, support groups, and loved ones. A multidisciplinary approach can provide comprehensive support and improve treatment outcomes.

- Ongoing Support: Ongoing support is crucial for managing compulsive behaviors and maintaining progress. Regular therapy sessions, participation in support groups, and communication with loved ones can provide ongoing encouragement and guidance.

- Self-Care: Incorporating self-care practices into your routine can enhance your overall well-being and support your treatment. Self-care can include activities such as exercise, mindfulness, creative pursuits, and relaxation techniques.

Conclusion

Seeking professional help is a critical step in the journey towards recovery from compulsive behaviors. Understanding the different types of therapy and counseling, medication options, and strategies for finding the right therapist or support group can empower individuals to make informed decisions about their treatment.

Therapeutic approaches such as CBT, ERP, ACT, DBT, and others offer effective strategies for managing compulsive behaviors and improving overall functioning. Medications, including SSRIs, TCAs, SNRIs, and others, can provide additional support in reducing the severity of these behaviors. Finding a qualified therapist or support group involves assessing your needs, considering qualifications and experience, and evaluating the fit and dynamics of the provider or group.

By taking proactive steps to seek help and build a support network, individuals can overcome the challenges posed by compulsive behaviors and work towards a healthier, more balanced future. With the right tools, techniques, and support, it is possible to achieve meaningful and lasting recovery.

Chapter 6: Cognitive-Behavioral Strategies

Introduction to Cognitive-Behavioral Therapy (CBT)

Cognitive-Behavioral Therapy (CBT) is one of the most widely used and empirically supported therapeutic approaches for treating a variety of mental health disorders, including compulsive behaviors. CBT is based on the premise that our thoughts, feelings, and behaviors are interconnected, and that changing negative thought patterns and behaviors can lead to improvements in emotional well-being and overall functioning.

1. Foundations of CBT

- The Cognitive Model: The cognitive model posits that our thoughts significantly influence our emotions and behaviors. Negative or irrational thoughts can lead to distressing emotions and maladaptive behaviors. By identifying and challenging these thoughts, we can change how we feel and behave.

- Behavioral Principles: Behavioral principles in CBT focus on how behaviors are learned and reinforced. Compulsive behaviors, for example, are often maintained through negative reinforcement, where the behavior reduces or avoids anxiety, thereby strengthening the compulsion.

2. Goals of CBT

- Symptom Reduction: The primary goal of CBT is to reduce symptoms of distress, such as anxiety and depression, by changing maladaptive thoughts and behaviors.

- Skill Building: CBT aims to equip individuals with skills to manage their thoughts, emotions, and behaviors more effectively, promoting long-term mental health and resilience.

- Improved Functioning: By addressing and modifying negative thought patterns and behaviors, CBT helps individuals improve their daily functioning and overall quality of life.

3. Structure of CBT

- Time-Limited and Structured: CBT is typically a short-term, structured therapy, with sessions usually lasting 12 to 20 weeks. The structured nature of CBT allows for focused and goal-oriented interventions.

- Collaborative Approach: CBT is a collaborative process between the therapist and the individual. The therapist provides guidance and support, while the individual actively participates in identifying and challenging negative thoughts and behaviors.

4. CBT Techniques

- Cognitive Restructuring: Cognitive restructuring involves identifying and challenging irrational or maladaptive thoughts and replacing them with more realistic and balanced thoughts.

- Behavioral Experiments: Behavioral experiments are practical exercises designed to test the validity of negative thoughts and beliefs. These experiments help individuals gather evidence and re-evaluate their assumptions.

- Exposure and Response Prevention (ERP): ERP is a specific technique used in CBT for anxiety and obsessive-compulsive disorder (OCD). It involves gradually exposing individuals to anxiety-provoking stimuli while preventing the compulsive response.

- Mindfulness and Relaxation Techniques: Mindfulness and relaxation techniques are often integrated into CBT to help individuals manage stress and anxiety.

Techniques for Identifying and Challenging Irrational Thoughts

IDENTIFYING AND CHALLENGING irrational thoughts is a core component of CBT. These thoughts, also known as cognitive distortions, can contribute to negative emotions and maladaptive behaviors. By learning to recognize and reframe these thoughts, individuals can reduce their emotional distress and improve their mental health.

1. Common Cognitive Distortions

- All-or-Nothing Thinking: Viewing situations in black-and-white terms, without recognizing the gray areas. For example, thinking, "If I don't succeed at everything, I'm a complete failure."

- Overgeneralization: Making broad, sweeping conclusions based on a single event. For example, believing, "I failed this test, so I'll never succeed in anything."

- Mental Filtering: Focusing solely on the negative aspects of a situation while ignoring the positive. For example, dwelling on a single criticism and ignoring the praise received.

- Disqualifying the Positive: Dismissing positive experiences or accomplishments as unimportant or invalid. For example, thinking, "Anyone could have done what I did; it's not a big deal."

- Jumping to Conclusions: Making negative assumptions without evidence. This includes mind reading (assuming others think negatively of you) and fortune telling (predicting negative outcomes).

- Catastrophizing: Exaggerating the importance of a negative event or outcome. For example, believing, "If I make a mistake, it will be a complete disaster."

- Emotional Reasoning: Assuming that negative emotions reflect reality. For example, thinking, "I feel anxious, so something bad must be happening."

- Should Statements: Imposing rigid expectations on oneself or others. For example, thinking, "I should always be perfect" or "People should always treat me kindly."

- Labeling and Mislabeling: Attaching a negative label to oneself or others. For example, calling oneself "a loser" after a setback.

- Personalization: Blaming oneself for events outside of one's control. For example, thinking, "It's my fault my friend is upset, even though I didn't do anything wrong."

2. Steps for Challenging Irrational Thoughts

- Identifying the Thought: The first step is to become aware of the irrational thought. This involves paying attention to moments of distress and recognizing the specific thoughts contributing to the negative emotions.

- Examining the Evidence: Evaluate the evidence for and against the irrational thought. Consider the facts and gather information to determine if the thought is based on reality.

- Alternative Explanations: Generate alternative, more balanced explanations for the situation. Consider other possible reasons for the event or outcome.

- Decatastrophizing: Assess the actual impact of the feared event. Consider the worst-case scenario and how you would cope with it, as well as the best-case and most likely scenarios.

- Reframing the Thought: Replace the irrational thought with a more realistic and balanced thought. Focus on evidence-based reasoning and positive self-talk.

3. Techniques for Challenging Irrational Thoughts

- Thought Records: Thought records are worksheets used to document irrational thoughts, the evidence for and against them, and alternative balanced thoughts. They help individuals systematically challenge cognitive distortions.

- Socratic Questioning: Socratic questioning involves asking oneself a series of guided questions to explore and challenge irrational thoughts. Questions may include, "What evidence do I have for this thought?" and "Are there alternative explanations?"

- Behavioral Experiments: Behavioral experiments involve testing the validity of irrational thoughts through real-life actions. For example, if someone believes they will fail at a task, they might attempt the task and observe the outcome.

- Cognitive Restructuring: Cognitive restructuring involves identifying and reframing irrational thoughts using logical reasoning. It helps individuals develop a more balanced and realistic perspective.

Practical Exercises for Behavior Modification

BEHAVIOR MODIFICATION is a key component of CBT, focusing on changing maladaptive behaviors through practical exercises and interventions. These exercises help individuals develop healthier habits, reduce distressing behaviors, and improve overall functioning.

1. Behavioral Activation

- Overview: Behavioral activation involves engaging in activities that are enjoyable or meaningful to counteract negative emotions and increase positive reinforcement. It is particularly effective for treating depression.

- Steps:

- Identify Activities: List activities that you find enjoyable or meaningful. These can include hobbies, social interactions, physical exercise, and self-care practices.

- Schedule Activities: Create a weekly schedule that includes these activities. Start with small, manageable goals and gradually increase the frequency and duration.

- Track Progress: Monitor your engagement in the activities and the impact on your mood and well-being. Adjust the schedule as needed to maintain consistency.

- Benefits: Behavioral activation helps individuals break the cycle of inactivity and negative emotions, promoting a sense of accomplishment and improving mood.

2. Exposure Therapy

- Overview: Exposure therapy involves gradually exposing individuals to feared stimuli or situations to reduce anxiety and avoidance behaviors. It is particularly effective for anxiety disorders and OCD.

- Steps:

- Identify Triggers: List situations or stimuli that trigger anxiety or compulsive behaviors.

- Develop a Hierarchy: Rank the triggers from least to most anxiety-provoking. Start with the least distressing and gradually work up to the most challenging.

- Gradual Exposure: Begin with the least anxiety-provoking trigger and expose yourself to it repeatedly until the anxiety decreases. Gradually progress to more challenging triggers.

- Response Prevention: During exposure, resist the urge to engage in avoidance or compulsive behaviors. This helps weaken the reinforcement of these behaviors.

- Benefits: Exposure therapy helps individuals confront their fears, reduce avoidance, and build resilience in managing anxiety.

3. Mindfulness and Relaxation Techniques

- Overview: Mindfulness and relaxation techniques help individuals manage stress and anxiety by promoting relaxation and present-moment awareness.

- Techniques:

- Mindfulness Meditation: Practice mindfulness meditation by focusing on your breath and observing your thoughts and sensations without judgment. Aim for 10-20 minutes of practice daily.

- Progressive Muscle Relaxation: Practice progressive muscle relaxation by tensing and relaxing different muscle groups in the body. This helps reduce physical tension and promote relaxation.

- Guided Imagery: Use guided imagery to visualize a peaceful and calming scene. This technique helps reduce stress and anxiety by creating a mental escape.

- Benefits: Mindfulness and relaxation techniques help individuals develop greater emotional regulation, reduce stress, and improve overall well-being.

4. Behavioral Contracts

- Overview: Behavioral contracts are written agreements between an individual and their therapist or support person, outlining specific behavior goals and consequences. They provide structure and accountability for behavior change.

- Steps:

- Identify Goals: Clearly define the behavior goals you want to achieve. These should be specific, measurable, achievable, relevant, and time-bound (SMART).

- Outline Consequences: Determine the positive and negative consequences for meeting or not meeting the behavior goals. Consequences should be meaningful and motivating.

- Monitor Progress: Regularly review and update the behavioral contract to track progress and make adjustments as needed.

- Benefits: Behavioral contracts provide clear expectations and accountability, increasing motivation and commitment to behavior change.

5. Problem-Solving Skills Training

- Overview: Problem-solving skills training helps individuals develop effective strategies for managing challenges and stressors. It involves identifying problems, generating solutions, and implementing action plans.

- Steps:

- Identify the Problem: Clearly define the problem you are facing. Break it down into smaller, manageable parts if needed.

- Generate Solutions: Brainstorm possible solutions to the problem. Consider different approaches and weigh the pros and cons of each.

- Implement an Action Plan: Choose the best solution and create a step-by-step action plan for implementing it. Set specific goals and timelines.

- Evaluate the Outcome: Assess the effectiveness of the solution and make adjustments if needed. Reflect on what worked well and what could be improved.

- Benefits: Problem-solving skills training enhances an individual's ability to cope with challenges, reduce stress, and improve overall problem-solving abilities.

6. Self-Monitoring and Tracking

- Overview: Self-monitoring involves regularly tracking thoughts, emotions, and behaviors to identify patterns and triggers. It provides valuable insights for behavior modification and cognitive restructuring.

- Steps:

- Identify Target Behaviors: Determine the specific thoughts, emotions, or behaviors you want to monitor. These should be relevant to your treatment goals.

- Create a Monitoring System: Use a journal, app, or worksheet to record your observations. Include details such as the time, situation, thoughts, emotions, and behaviors.

- Analyze Patterns: Review your records to identify patterns and triggers. Consider how your thoughts and behaviors are connected to your emotions.

- Implement Changes: Use the insights gained from self-monitoring to make targeted changes in your thoughts and behaviors. Track your progress and adjust as needed.

- Benefits: Self-monitoring increases self-awareness and provides valuable data for identifying and modifying maladaptive thoughts and behaviors.

Detailed Examples and Case Studies

TO ILLUSTRATE THE APPLICATION of cognitive-behavioral strategies, let's explore detailed examples and case studies of individuals using these techniques to address compulsive behaviors.

Case Study 1: Overcoming Obsessive-Compulsive Disorder (OCD)

BACKGROUND: SARAH IS a 32-year-old woman who has been struggling with OCD for several years. Her compulsions primarily involve excessive handwashing and checking behaviors. She spends several hours each day washing her hands and repeatedly checking locks and appliances, which significantly interferes with her daily life and responsibilities.

Treatment Plan:

1. Cognitive Restructuring:

- Identifying Irrational Thoughts: Sarah identified the irrational thought, "If I don't wash my hands repeatedly, I will get sick and harm others."

- Examining the Evidence: Sarah examined the evidence for and against this thought. She acknowledged that while good hygiene is important, excessive handwashing is not necessary to prevent illness.

- Reframing the Thought: Sarah replaced the irrational thought with a more balanced thought: "Washing my hands once is sufficient to maintain hygiene and prevent illness."

2. Exposure and Response Prevention (ERP):

- Developing a Hierarchy: Sarah created a hierarchy of her anxiety-provoking situations, ranking them from least to most distressing. The hierarchy included tasks such as touching doorknobs without washing her hands immediately and reducing the frequency of checking behaviors.

- Gradual Exposure: Sarah began with the least anxiety-provoking task, touching doorknobs without immediately washing her hands. She practiced this exposure repeatedly until her anxiety decreased.

- Response Prevention: During exposure, Sarah resisted the urge to wash her hands. Over time, she progressed to more challenging tasks, such as reducing the frequency of checking behaviors.

3. Mindfulness and Relaxation Techniques:

- Mindfulness Meditation: Sarah practiced mindfulness meditation daily, focusing on her breath and observing her thoughts without judgment. This helped her manage anxiety and reduce the impact of intrusive thoughts.

- Progressive Muscle Relaxation: Sarah used progressive muscle relaxation techniques to reduce physical tension and promote relaxation, particularly before engaging in exposure exercises.

Outcome: Over the course of several months, Sarah experienced significant reductions in her compulsive behaviors and anxiety. She was able to complete daily tasks more efficiently and engage in activities she previously avoided. Sarah continued to use the skills she learned in therapy to manage her symptoms and maintain her progress.

Case Study 2: Addressing Compulsive Hoarding

BACKGROUND: MARK IS a 45-year-old man who has been struggling with compulsive hoarding for over a decade. His home is filled with items he cannot bring himself to discard, including old newspapers, clothing, and broken appliances. The clutter has reached a point where most rooms are unusable, and his living conditions are hazardous.

Treatment Plan:

1. Cognitive Restructuring:

- Identifying Irrational Thoughts: Mark identified the irrational thought, "I might need these items in the future, and getting rid of them would be a mistake."

- Examining the Evidence: Mark examined the evidence for and against this thought. He acknowledged that many of the items had not been used in years and were unlikely to be needed.

- Reframing the Thought: Mark replaced the irrational thought with a more balanced thought: "I can let go of items that no longer serve a purpose. Keeping my home organized and safe is more important."

2. Behavioral Activation:

- Identifying Activities: Mark identified activities that were meaningful to him, such as spending time with family and working on hobbies. He recognized that decluttering his home would enable him to engage in these activities more fully.

- Scheduling Activities: Mark created a weekly schedule that included time for decluttering and organizing his home. He set specific goals for each session, such as clearing a specific area or sorting through a certain number of items.

3. Behavioral Experiments:

- Testing Assumptions: Mark conducted behavioral experiments to test his assumptions about the necessity of keeping certain items. For example, he temporarily placed items in storage to see if he needed them within a set period.

- Evaluating Outcomes: Mark evaluated the outcomes of these experiments and found that he did not miss or need most of the items he stored. This evidence helped him feel more comfortable letting go of unnecessary possessions.

4. Support and Accountability:

- Enlisting Support: Mark enlisted the support of a trusted friend to help him with the decluttering process. This friend provided encouragement, accountability, and practical assistance.

- Joining a Support Group: Mark joined a support group for individuals with compulsive hoarding. The group provided a sense of community, shared experiences, and additional motivation for making progress.

Outcome: Over time, Mark made significant progress in decluttering and organizing his home. He was able to create a safer and more functional living space, which improved his quality of life and allowed him to engage in activities he enjoyed. Mark continued to use the skills he learned in therapy to maintain his progress and prevent relapse.

Case Study 3: Managing Compulsive Eating

BACKGROUND: EMILY IS a 28-year-old woman who has been struggling with compulsive eating since her teenage years. During periods of stress, she turns to food for comfort and often engages in binge-eating episodes. These episodes are followed by feelings of guilt and shame, perpetuating a cycle of emotional eating.

Treatment Plan:

1. Cognitive Restructuring:

- Identifying Irrational Thoughts: Emily identified the irrational thought, "Eating is the only way I can cope with my stress."

- Examining the Evidence: Emily examined the evidence for and against this thought. She acknowledged that while eating provided temporary comfort, it did not address the underlying stress and often led to negative consequences.

- Reframing the Thought: Emily replaced the irrational thought with a more balanced thought: "There are healthier ways to cope with stress that can provide lasting relief."

2. Behavioral Activation:

- Identifying Activities: Emily identified activities that helped her relax and reduce stress, such as exercise, journaling, and spending time with friends. She recognized that engaging in these activities could provide healthier coping mechanisms.

- Scheduling Activities: Emily created a weekly schedule that included time for these stress-relieving activities. She made a commitment to prioritize self-care and engage in these activities regularly.

3. Mindfulness and Relaxation Techniques:

- Mindfulness Meditation: Emily practiced mindfulness meditation daily, focusing on her breath and observing her thoughts and cravings without judgment. This helped her become more aware of her emotional triggers for eating.

- Guided Imagery: Emily used guided imagery to visualize herself managing stress in healthy ways. This technique helped her reinforce positive coping strategies and reduce the urge to engage in compulsive eating.

4. Behavioral Experiments:

- Testing Alternatives: Emily conducted behavioral experiments to test alternative coping strategies. For example, when she felt the urge to binge eat, she tried engaging in a different activity, such as going for a walk or calling a friend.

- Evaluating Outcomes: Emily evaluated the outcomes of these experiments and found that alternative coping strategies were effective in reducing stress and preventing binge-eating episodes.

Outcome: Over the course of several months, Emily experienced significant reductions in her compulsive eating behaviors and emotional distress. She developed healthier ways to cope with stress and improved her overall well-being. Emily continued to use the skills she learned in therapy to maintain her progress and prevent relapse.

Conclusion

Cognitive-behavioral strategies offer effective tools for managing and overcoming compulsive behaviors. By understanding the foundations of CBT, learning techniques for identifying and challenging irrational thoughts, and engaging in practical exercises for behavior modification, individuals can make meaningful and lasting changes in their lives.

Through cognitive restructuring, exposure therapy, behavioral activation, mindfulness, and other CBT techniques, individuals can develop healthier thought patterns and behaviors. These strategies empower individuals to take control of their mental health, reduce distressing symptoms, and improve their overall quality of life.

The case studies presented in this chapter illustrate the application of cognitive-behavioral strategies in real-life scenarios. They highlight the potential for significant improvement and recovery when individuals actively engage in the therapeutic process and utilize the skills they learn in therapy.

By incorporating cognitive-behavioral strategies into their treatment plans, individuals can achieve meaningful and lasting recovery from compulsive behaviors. With the right tools, techniques, and support, it is possible to overcome the challenges posed by compulsive behaviors and work towards a healthier, more balanced future.

Chapter 7: Mindfulness and Meditation

The Role of Mindfulness in Managing Compulsive Behaviors

Mindfulness is a mental practice that involves focusing one's attention on the present moment, with an attitude of openness, curiosity, and non-judgment. It is derived from ancient meditation practices, particularly those rooted in Buddhist traditions, but has been adapted and incorporated into modern psychological treatments for various mental health issues, including compulsive behaviors.

1. Understanding Mindfulness

- Definition: Mindfulness is the practice of bringing one's attention to the present moment and observing thoughts, feelings, and sensations without judgment. It involves acknowledging whatever arises in awareness with acceptance.

- Principles: The core principles of mindfulness include present-moment awareness, acceptance, non-judgment, and letting go of attachment to thoughts and emotions. These principles help individuals develop a balanced and detached perspective towards their experiences.

2. Mechanisms of Mindfulness in Managing Compulsive Behaviors

- Awareness and Identification: Mindfulness enhances self-awareness, enabling individuals to recognize the onset of compulsive urges and behaviors. This awareness is the first step in managing and modifying these behaviors.

- Detachment from Thoughts: By observing thoughts and emotions without judgment, mindfulness helps individuals detach from the compulsive thought patterns that drive their behaviors. This detachment reduces the power of these thoughts and diminishes their impact.

- Reduction of Automaticity: Compulsive behaviors are often automatic responses to anxiety or distress. Mindfulness interrupts this automaticity by bringing conscious awareness to these responses, allowing individuals to make deliberate choices rather than acting on impulse.

- Emotional Regulation: Mindfulness practices enhance emotional regulation, helping individuals manage the anxiety, stress, and other emotions that often trigger compulsive behaviors. Improved emotional regulation reduces the likelihood of resorting to compulsions as a coping mechanism.

- Increased Tolerance for Discomfort: Mindfulness teaches individuals to tolerate discomfort and distress without needing to escape or avoid it. This increased tolerance reduces the reliance on compulsive behaviors to alleviate discomfort.

3. Research Evidence

- Effectiveness: Numerous studies have demonstrated the effectiveness of mindfulness-based interventions in reducing compulsive behaviors. Research has shown that mindfulness practices can significantly reduce symptoms of OCD, binge eating, and other compulsive behaviors.

- Brain Changes: Neuroimaging studies have shown that mindfulness practices can lead to structural and functional changes in the brain, particularly in areas involved in emotional regulation, self-awareness, and cognitive control. These changes support the ability to manage compulsive behaviors more effectively.

Meditation Techniques to Enhance Self-Awareness and Control

MEDITATION IS A KEY component of mindfulness practice, offering various techniques to enhance self-awareness, control, and emotional regulation. Different meditation techniques can be tailored to individual preferences and needs, providing a range of tools for managing compulsive behaviors.

1. Mindfulness Meditation

- Overview: Mindfulness meditation involves focusing attention on the present moment, typically by observing the breath, bodily sensations, or a specific point of focus. The goal is to cultivate awareness and acceptance of whatever arises in the mind.

- Steps:

- Find a Comfortable Position: Sit or lie down in a comfortable position, ensuring your back is straight but relaxed.

- Focus on the Breath: Bring your attention to your breath, noticing the sensations of inhaling and exhaling. Observe the breath without trying to change it.

- Observe Thoughts and Sensations: As thoughts, feelings, or sensations arise, observe them without judgment. Acknowledge their presence and gently return your focus to the breath.

- Practice Regularly: Aim to practice mindfulness meditation for at least 10-20 minutes daily. Consistency is key to developing mindfulness skills.

- Benefits: Mindfulness meditation enhances self-awareness, reduces automatic reactions, and improves emotional regulation. It helps individuals observe their compulsive thoughts and urges without being controlled by them.

2. Body Scan Meditation

- Overview: Body scan meditation involves systematically focusing attention on different parts of the body, from head to toe. This practice promotes awareness of bodily sensations and helps release physical tension.

- Steps:

- Find a Comfortable Position: Lie down or sit in a comfortable position. Close your eyes if it feels comfortable.

- Focus on the Breath: Take a few deep breaths to center yourself and bring your attention to the present moment.

- Scan the Body: Begin at the top of your head and gradually move your attention down through your body. Notice any sensations, tension, or areas of discomfort.

- Observe Without Judgment: Observe each area of the body without judgment. If your mind wanders, gently bring your focus back to the body scan.

- Practice Regularly: Aim to practice body scan meditation for at least 20-30 minutes a few times a week.

- Benefits: Body scan meditation enhances bodily awareness, reduces physical tension, and promotes relaxation. It helps individuals become more attuned to the physical manifestations of their compulsive behaviors and develop greater control over their bodily responses.

3. Loving-Kindness Meditation

- Overview: Loving-kindness meditation, also known as Metta meditation, involves cultivating feelings of compassion and love towards oneself and others. This practice promotes positive emotions and reduces negative self-judgment.

- Steps:

- Find a Comfortable Position: Sit in a comfortable position with your eyes closed. Take a few deep breaths to center yourself.

- Generate Loving-Kindness: Begin by directing loving-kindness towards yourself. Repeat phrases such as, "May I be happy. May I be healthy. May I be safe. May I live with ease."

- Extend to Others: Gradually extend loving-kindness to others, starting with loved ones, then acquaintances, and finally all beings. Repeat similar phrases for each group.

- Practice Regularly: Aim to practice loving-kindness meditation for at least 10-15 minutes daily.

- Benefits: Loving-kindness meditation enhances positive emotions, reduces self-criticism, and promotes feelings of connectedness. It helps individuals develop greater self-compassion and reduce the negative emotions that often drive compulsive behaviors.

4. Breath Awareness Meditation

- Overview: Breath awareness meditation involves focusing attention on the breath as it naturally flows in and out of the body. This practice helps cultivate mindfulness and present-moment awareness.

- Steps:

- Find a Comfortable Position: Sit or lie down in a comfortable position. Close your eyes if it feels comfortable.

- Focus on the Breath: Bring your attention to your breath, noticing the sensations of inhaling and exhaling. Observe the breath without trying to change it.

- Count the Breaths: To maintain focus, count each breath. Inhale and count "one," exhale and count "two," and so on, up to ten. Then start again from one.

- Practice Regularly: Aim to practice breath awareness meditation for at least 10-20 minutes daily.

- Benefits: Breath awareness meditation enhances concentration, reduces mind-wandering, and promotes relaxation. It helps individuals anchor their attention in the present moment and reduce the influence of compulsive thoughts and urges.

5. Guided Imagery

- Overview: Guided imagery involves using the imagination to visualize calming and positive scenes or experiences. This practice helps reduce stress and anxiety by creating a mental escape.

- Steps:

- Find a Comfortable Position: Sit or lie down in a comfortable position. Close your eyes if it feels comfortable.

- Choose a Scene: Choose a calming and positive scene to visualize, such as a beach, forest, or garden. Imagine this scene in vivid detail, engaging all your senses.

- Guided Script: Follow a guided script or recording that leads you through the visualization. Focus on the sights, sounds, smells, and sensations of the scene.

- Practice Regularly: Aim to practice guided imagery for at least 10-15 minutes a few times a week.

- Benefits: Guided imagery reduces stress and anxiety, promotes relaxation, and enhances positive emotions. It provides a mental break from compulsive thoughts and behaviors, creating a sense of calm and well-being.

Integrating Mindfulness into Daily Routines

INTEGRATING MINDFULNESS into daily routines can help individuals develop a consistent practice and experience the benefits of mindfulness throughout their day. Practical strategies for incorporating mindfulness into everyday activities can make mindfulness accessible and sustainable.

1. Mindful Breathing

- Overview: Mindful breathing involves paying attention to the breath during everyday activities. This practice can be done at any time and in any place.

- Steps:

- Choose a Moment: Select specific moments during your day to practice mindful breathing, such as when you wake up, before meals, or before going to bed.

- Focus on the Breath: Take a few deep breaths and bring your attention to the sensations of breathing. Notice the rise and fall of your chest or abdomen.

- Observe Without Judgment: Observe your breath without judgment. If your mind wanders, gently bring your focus back to the breath.

- Benefits: Mindful breathing enhances present-moment awareness, reduces stress, and promotes relaxation. It provides a simple and accessible way to incorporate mindfulness into daily life.

2. Mindful Eating

- Overview: Mindful eating involves paying attention to the experience of eating, including the taste, texture, and aroma of food. This practice promotes a healthier relationship with food and reduces mindless eating.

- Steps:

- Choose a Meal: Select one meal or snack each day to practice mindful eating.

- Focus on the Experience: Before eating, take a moment to appreciate the food. Notice its appearance, aroma, and texture.

- Eat Slowly: Eat slowly and savor each bite. Pay attention to the taste, texture, and sensations of eating.

- Observe Hunger and Fullness: Notice your hunger and fullness cues. Eat until you are satisfied, but not overly full.

- Benefits: Mindful eating enhances the enjoyment of food, promotes healthier eating habits, and reduces overeating. It helps individuals develop a more conscious and intentional relationship with food.

3. Mindful Walking

- Overview: Mindful walking involves paying attention to the sensations of walking and the environment around you. This practice can be done during daily walks or as a specific mindfulness exercise.

- Steps:

- Choose a Route: Select a route for your mindful walk, whether it's in nature, a park, or around your neighborhood.

- Focus on Sensations: Pay attention to the sensations of walking, such as the movement of your legs, the feel of your feet on the ground, and your breath.

- Observe the Environment: Notice the sights, sounds, and smells around you. Engage your senses and observe without judgment.

- Practice Regularly: Aim to practice mindful walking for at least 10-20 minutes a few times a week.

- Benefits: Mindful walking enhances present-moment awareness, reduces stress, and promotes physical and mental well-being. It provides an opportunity to connect with nature and experience the benefits of physical activity.

4. Mindful Listening

- Overview: Mindful listening involves paying full attention to sounds and conversations without judgment or distraction. This practice enhances communication and deepens connections with others.

- Steps:

- Choose a Moment: Select moments during your day to practice mindful listening, such as during conversations or while listening to music.

- Focus on Sounds: Pay attention to the sounds around you. Notice the nuances of different sounds, such as the tone, pitch, and rhythm.

- Observe Without Judgment: Observe the sounds without judgment. If your mind wanders, gently bring your focus back to the sounds.

- **Benefits**: Mindful listening enhances communication skills, deepens connections with others, and promotes present-moment awareness. It helps individuals become more attentive and engaged listeners.

5. Mindful Journaling

- Overview: Mindful journaling involves writing about thoughts, feelings, and experiences with an attitude of openness and non-judgment. This practice promotes self-reflection and emotional processing.

- Steps:

- Choose a Time: Select a specific time each day to practice mindful journaling, such as in the morning or before bed.

- Write Freely: Write about your thoughts, feelings, and experiences without censoring or judging yourself. Allow your writing to flow naturally.

- Reflect: Reflect on what you have written and observe any patterns or insights. Use your journal as a tool for self-discovery and emotional processing.

- Benefits: Mindful journaling enhances self-awareness, promotes emotional processing, and provides a space for self-expression. It helps individuals gain insights into their thoughts and behaviors.

Detailed Examples and Case Studies

TO ILLUSTRATE THE APPLICATION of mindfulness and meditation techniques, let's explore detailed examples and case studies of individuals using these practices to manage compulsive behaviors.

Case Study 1: Managing OCD with Mindfulness Meditation

BACKGROUND: JOHN IS a 35-year-old man who has been struggling with OCD for several years. His compulsions primarily involve excessive checking behaviors, such as repeatedly checking locks and appliances. These behaviors significantly interfere with his daily life and responsibilities.

Mindfulness Practice:

1. MINDFULNESS MEDITATION:

- Daily Practice: John committed to practicing mindfulness meditation for 20 minutes every morning. He found a quiet space, sat comfortably, and focused on his breath.

- Observing Thoughts: During meditation, John observed his intrusive thoughts without judgment. He acknowledged their presence and gently returned his focus to his breath.

- Non-Judgmental Awareness: John practiced non-judgmental awareness by accepting his thoughts and feelings without trying to change them. This helped him develop a more detached perspective towards his compulsive thoughts.

2. Integrating Mindfulness into Daily Routines:

- Mindful Breathing: John incorporated mindful breathing into his daily routines, such as during his commute to work and before meals. This helped him stay grounded and present throughout the day.

- Mindful Walking: John practiced mindful walking during his lunch breaks, paying attention to the sensations of walking and the environment around him. This provided a mental break and reduced his anxiety.

Outcome: Over several months, John experienced significant reductions in his compulsive checking behaviors and anxiety. Mindfulness meditation helped him observe his intrusive thoughts without being controlled by them, and integrating mindfulness into his daily routines promoted present-moment awareness and emotional regulation. John continued to use mindfulness practices to manage his OCD and maintain his progress.

Case Study 2: Addressing Compulsive Eating with Mindful Eating

BACKGROUND: LISA IS a 29-year-old woman who has been struggling with compulsive eating for several years. She often engages in binge-eating episodes during periods of stress, which are followed by feelings of guilt and shame.

Mindfulness Practice:

1. MINDFUL EATING:

- Choosing a Meal: Lisa committed to practicing mindful eating during dinner each evening. She prepared her meals with care and attention, selecting foods she enjoyed.

- Focusing on the Experience: Before eating, Lisa took a moment to appreciate the appearance, aroma, and texture of the food. She ate slowly and savored each bite, paying attention to the taste and sensations of eating.

- Observing Hunger and Fullness: Lisa tuned into her hunger and fullness cues, eating until she was satisfied but not overly full. She practiced non-judgmental awareness of her body's signals.

2. Mindfulness Meditation:

- Daily Practice: Lisa practiced mindfulness meditation for 15 minutes each morning. She focused on her breath and observed her thoughts and cravings without judgment.

- Emotional Awareness: Lisa used mindfulness meditation to become more aware of her emotional triggers for eating. She acknowledged her emotions and developed healthier ways to cope with stress.

Outcome: Over several months, Lisa experienced significant reductions in her compulsive eating behaviors and emotional distress. Mindful eating helped her develop a healthier relationship with food, and mindfulness meditation enhanced her emotional awareness and regulation. Lisa continued to use mindfulness practices to manage her compulsive eating and maintain her progress.

Case Study 3: Enhancing Emotional Regulation with Loving-Kindness Meditation

BACKGROUND: MARK IS a 42-year-old man who has been struggling with compulsive behaviors related to workaholism. He often works excessively to cope with feelings of inadequacy and stress, which has led to burnout and strained relationships.

Mindfulness Practice:

1. LOVING-KINDNESS Meditation:

- Daily Practice: Mark committed to practicing loving-kindness meditation for 15 minutes each evening. He found a quiet space, sat comfortably, and closed his eyes.

- Generating Loving-Kindness: Mark began by directing loving-kindness towards himself, repeating phrases such as, "May I be happy. May I be healthy. May I be safe. May I live with ease."

- Extending to Others: Mark gradually extended loving-kindness to others, starting with loved ones, then acquaintances, and finally all beings. He repeated similar phrases for each group.

2. Mindfulness Meditation:

- Daily Practice: Mark practiced mindfulness meditation for 20 minutes each morning. He focused on his breath and observed his thoughts and emotions without judgment.

- Emotional Awareness: Mark used mindfulness meditation to become more aware of his emotional triggers for workaholism. He acknowledged his feelings of inadequacy and developed healthier ways to cope with stress.

Outcome: Over several months, Mark experienced significant reductions in his compulsive work behaviors and emotional distress. Loving-kindness meditation enhanced his self-compassion and positive emotions, while mindfulness meditation improved his emotional regulation. Mark continued to use mindfulness practices to manage his workaholism and maintain his progress.

Conclusion

Mindfulness and meditation offer powerful tools for managing and overcoming compulsive behaviors. By understanding the role of mindfulness in enhancing self-awareness, emotional regulation, and present-moment awareness, individuals can develop effective strategies for managing their compulsions.

Various meditation techniques, including mindfulness meditation, body scan meditation, loving-kindness meditation, breath awareness meditation, and guided imagery, provide a range of tools for enhancing self-awareness and control. Integrating mindfulness into daily routines through practices such as mindful breathing, mindful eating, mindful walking, mindful listening, and mindful journaling can make mindfulness accessible and sustainable.

The detailed examples and case studies presented in this chapter illustrate the application of mindfulness and meditation techniques in real-life scenarios. They highlight the potential for significant improvement and recovery when individuals actively engage in mindfulness practices and integrate them into their daily lives.

By incorporating mindfulness and meditation into their treatment plans, individuals can achieve meaningful and lasting recovery from compulsive behaviors. With the right tools, techniques, and support, it is possible to overcome the challenges posed by compulsive behaviors and work towards a healthier, more balanced future.

Chapter 8: Building Healthy Habits

Strategies for Replacing Compulsive Behaviors with Positive Habits

Compulsive behaviors often emerge as maladaptive coping mechanisms for managing stress, anxiety, or other emotional challenges. Replacing these behaviors with positive habits can significantly enhance an individual's quality of life and overall well-being. The key to this transformation lies in understanding the underlying triggers, identifying healthier alternatives, and systematically integrating these alternatives into daily routines.

1. Understanding the Triggers

- Identifying Triggers: The first step in replacing compulsive behaviors is to identify the triggers that prompt them. Triggers can be emotional (e.g., stress, anxiety, boredom), situational (e.g., specific places or times of day), or cognitive (e.g., certain thoughts or memories).

- Journaling and Monitoring: Keeping a journal to track when and where compulsive behaviors occur can help identify patterns and triggers. Noting the circumstances, thoughts, and feelings associated with the behavior provides valuable insights.

2. Choosing Healthy Alternatives

- Positive Coping Mechanisms: Once triggers are identified, the next step is to choose positive coping mechanisms to replace the compulsive behaviors. These alternatives should address the same needs or provide similar relief. Examples include:

- Physical Activity: Exercise can be a powerful alternative to compulsive behaviors, as it reduces stress, improves mood, and promotes physical health.

- Mindfulness and Relaxation: Practices such as mindfulness meditation, deep breathing exercises, and yoga can help manage stress and anxiety.

- Creative Outlets: Engaging in creative activities such as drawing, writing, or playing music can provide an emotional release and distraction from compulsive urges.

- Social Support: Connecting with friends, family, or support groups can offer emotional support and reduce feelings of isolation.

- Healthy Hobbies: Developing new hobbies or interests can provide a sense of purpose and fulfillment, diverting attention from compulsive behaviors.

3. Gradual Integration

- Small Steps: Gradual integration of positive habits is more sustainable than attempting drastic changes. Start by replacing the compulsive behavior with a positive alternative for a short duration and gradually increase the time and frequency.

- Habit Stacking: Habit stacking involves pairing a new, positive habit with an existing routine. For example, if you have a compulsive habit of checking your phone frequently, you might replace it with a brief mindfulness practice each time you reach for your phone.

- Routine Development: Developing a structured daily routine that incorporates positive habits can create stability and reduce the likelihood of reverting to compulsive behaviors.

4. Creating a Supportive Environment

- Physical Environment: Modify your physical environment to reduce triggers and facilitate positive habits. This might include decluttering spaces associated with compulsive behaviors or setting up a dedicated area for exercise or mindfulness practices.

- Social Environment: Surround yourself with supportive individuals who encourage your positive habits and provide accountability. Sharing your goals with friends or family can help reinforce your commitment.

Setting Realistic Goals and Tracking Progress

SETTING REALISTIC GOALS and tracking progress are essential components of building and maintaining healthy habits. Goals provide direction and motivation, while tracking progress helps maintain accountability and celebrate achievements.

1. Setting Realistic Goals

- SMART Goals: Ensure that your goals are Specific, Measurable, Achievable, Relevant, and Time-bound (SMART). This framework helps create clear and attainable objectives.

- Specific: Clearly define what you want to achieve. For example, instead of setting a vague goal like "exercise more," specify "exercise for 30 minutes, three times a week."

- Measurable: Establish criteria to track your progress. This could be the number of minutes spent exercising or the number of pages read each week.

- Achievable: Set goals that are challenging yet attainable. Consider your current capabilities and resources when setting goals.

- Relevant: Ensure that your goals align with your values and long-term objectives. Ask yourself why the goal is important and how it contributes to your overall well-being.

- Time-bound: Set a deadline or timeframe for achieving your goals. This adds a sense of urgency and helps maintain focus.

2. Breaking Down Goals

- Short-Term and Long-Term Goals: Divide your goals into short-term and long-term objectives. Short-term goals provide immediate targets to work towards, while long-term goals offer a broader vision.

- Actionable Steps: Break down each goal into smaller, actionable steps. This makes the goal more manageable and reduces the likelihood of feeling overwhelmed.

3. Tracking Progress

- Journaling: Keep a journal to document your progress, noting achievements, challenges, and reflections. Journaling provides a record of your journey and offers insights into patterns and areas for improvement.

- Progress Charts: Use progress charts or graphs to visually track your achievements. This visual representation can be motivating and help you see your progress over time.

- Apps and Tools: Utilize apps and tools designed for goal tracking and habit formation. These digital tools can provide reminders, track progress, and offer encouragement.

4. Celebrating Achievements

- Milestone Celebrations: Celebrate milestones and achievements along the way. Acknowledging progress, no matter how small, reinforces positive behavior and boosts motivation.

- Rewards: Set up a reward system for achieving goals. Rewards can be small treats, activities you enjoy, or other incentives that motivate you to stay on track.

The Importance of Consistency and Patience

BUILDING HEALTHY HABITS requires consistency and patience. It is a gradual process that involves persistence, resilience, and a willingness to learn from setbacks.

1. Consistency

- Regular Practice: Consistency is key to habit formation. Regular practice helps embed new behaviors into your daily routine, making them more automatic over time.

- Daily Commitment: Make a daily commitment to your new habits, even if it's just a small effort. Consistent, small actions are more effective than sporadic, larger efforts.

- Overcoming Obstacles: Anticipate and plan for potential obstacles. Develop strategies to stay consistent, such as adjusting your schedule, seeking support, or using reminders.

2. Patience

- Realistic Expectations: Understand that building new habits takes time. Avoid setting unrealistic expectations or becoming discouraged by slow progress.

- Embracing the Process: Focus on the process rather than the outcome. Embrace the journey of self-improvement and the gradual changes that come with it.

- Learning from Setbacks: Recognize that setbacks are a natural part of the process. Instead of viewing them as failures, see them as opportunities to learn and grow. Reflect on what went wrong and how you can adjust your approach.

3. Resilience and Adaptability

- Staying Resilient: Building healthy habits requires resilience in the face of challenges. Stay committed to your goals, even when progress is slow or obstacles arise.

- Adapting to Change: Be flexible and adaptable in your approach. Life circumstances may change, requiring adjustments to your routine or goals. Stay open to change and find ways to adapt while maintaining your commitment.

4. Support Systems

- Accountability Partners: Find an accountability partner who can provide support, encouragement, and accountability. This could be a friend, family member, or mentor.

- Support Groups: Join support groups or communities that share similar goals. These groups can offer valuable insights, motivation, and a sense of belonging.

- Professional Guidance: Seek guidance from professionals, such as therapists or coaches, who can provide expert advice and support in building healthy habits.

Detailed Examples and Case Studies

TO ILLUSTRATE THE APPLICATION of strategies for building healthy habits, let's explore detailed examples and case studies of individuals who have successfully replaced compulsive behaviors with positive habits, set realistic goals, and maintained consistency and patience throughout the process.

Case Study 1: Replacing Compulsive Shopping with Mindful Spending

BACKGROUND: EMILY IS a 34-year-old woman who has been struggling with compulsive shopping for several years. She often buys unnecessary items to cope with stress and emotions, leading to financial problems and clutter.

Strategies and Goals:

1. IDENTIFYING TRIGGERS: Emily identified that she often felt the urge to shop when she was stressed, bored, or seeking validation. She kept a journal to track her emotions and triggers.

2. Choosing Healthy Alternatives:

- Mindful Spending: Emily decided to replace compulsive shopping with mindful spending. She committed to only buying items that she genuinely needed or that brought long-term value.

- Stress Management: Emily incorporated stress management techniques such as mindfulness meditation, exercise, and journaling into her daily routine to address her emotional triggers.

3. Setting Realistic Goals:

- Short-Term Goal: Reduce impulsive purchases by 50% within the first month.

- Long-Term Goal: Achieve financial stability and reduce debt by 30% within six months.

4. Tracking Progress:

- Spending Journal: Emily kept a spending journal to track her purchases, noting the reasons for each purchase and whether it aligned with her mindful spending goals.

- Financial Tracking: She used a financial tracking app to monitor her expenses and savings, setting monthly budgets and financial goals.

5. Celebrating Achievements:

- Milestones: Emily celebrated milestones such as achieving her monthly budget goals and reducing debt. She rewarded herself with non-monetary treats such as a relaxing day at home or a fun activity with friends.

Outcome: Over several months, Emily successfully replaced her compulsive shopping habits with mindful spending. She achieved her financial goals, reduced debt, and gained greater control over her spending. The combination of mindfulness practices, goal setting, and consistent tracking helped her maintain her progress and build healthier financial habits.

Case Study 2: Replacing Compulsive Eating with Healthy Nutrition and Exercise

BACKGROUND: JOHN IS a 45-year-old man who has been struggling with compulsive eating for many years. He often turns to food for comfort during stressful times, leading to weight gain and health issues.

Strategies and Goals:

1. IDENTIFYING TRIGGERS: John identified that he often ate compulsively when he felt stressed, lonely, or bored. He kept a food journal to track his eating patterns and triggers.

2. Choosing Healthy Alternatives:

- Healthy Nutrition: John decided to replace compulsive eating with healthy nutrition. He committed to planning balanced meals and choosing nutritious foods.

- Exercise Routine: John incorporated regular exercise into his daily routine to manage stress and improve his physical health. He started with daily walks and gradually added strength training and cardio exercises.

3. Setting Realistic Goals:

- Short-Term Goal: Reduce binge-eating episodes to once a week within the first month.

- Long-Term Goal: Achieve a healthy weight and improve overall health within six months.

4. Tracking Progress:

- Food Journal: John continued to keep a food journal to monitor his eating habits and make adjustments as needed.

- Fitness Tracking: He used a fitness tracking app to log his workouts, track his progress, and set new fitness goals.

5. Celebrating Achievements:

- Milestones: John celebrated milestones such as reaching his fitness goals and maintaining healthy eating habits. He rewarded himself with non-food treats such as new workout gear or a fun outing.

Outcome: Over several months, John successfully replaced his compulsive eating habits with healthy nutrition and exercise. He achieved his weight loss goals, improved his physical health, and developed a healthier relationship with food. The combination of healthy alternatives, goal setting, and consistent tracking helped him maintain his progress and build sustainable healthy habits.

Case Study 3: Replacing Compulsive Internet Use with Productive Activities

BACKGROUND: SARAH IS a 28-year-old woman who has been struggling with compulsive internet use, particularly social media and online gaming. This behavior has negatively impacted her productivity and social life.

Strategies and Goals:

1. IDENTIFYING TRIGGERS: Sarah identified that she often turned to the internet when she felt bored, anxious, or seeking social validation. She used a digital well-being app to track her internet usage and identify patterns.

2. Choosing Healthy Alternatives:

- Productive Activities: Sarah decided to replace compulsive internet use with productive activities such as reading, learning new skills, and engaging in hobbies.

- Social Engagement: She committed to spending more time with friends and family in person, joining social clubs, and participating in community events.

3. Setting Realistic Goals:

- Short-Term Goal: Reduce daily internet use by 50% within the first month.

- Long-Term Goal: Achieve a balanced and productive lifestyle with limited internet use within six months.

4. Tracking Progress:

- Digital Well-Being App: Sarah continued to use the digital well-being app to monitor her internet usage and set daily limits.

- Activity Log: She kept an activity log to track her productive activities and social engagements, noting the positive impacts on her well-being.

5. Celebrating Achievements:

- Milestones: Sarah celebrated milestones such as achieving her daily internet usage goals and engaging in new hobbies. She rewarded herself with experiences such as a weekend getaway or a special event with friends.

Outcome: Over several months, Sarah successfully replaced her compulsive internet use with productive activities and social engagement. She achieved a balanced lifestyle, improved her productivity, and enhanced her social life. The combination of healthy alternatives, goal setting, and consistent tracking helped her maintain her progress and build sustainable healthy habits.

Conclusion

Building healthy habits is a transformative process that involves replacing compulsive behaviors with positive alternatives, setting realistic goals, and maintaining consistency and patience. By understanding the underlying triggers, choosing healthier alternatives, and integrating these alternatives into daily routines, individuals can significantly enhance their quality of life and overall well-being.

Setting realistic goals using the SMART framework, breaking down goals into actionable steps, and tracking progress through journaling, progress charts, and digital tools provide direction and motivation. Celebrating achievements and setting up a reward system reinforce positive behavior and boost motivation.

Consistency and patience are essential components of building healthy habits. Regular practice, daily commitment, and resilience in the face of challenges ensure the sustainability of new habits. Support systems, including accountability partners, support groups, and professional guidance, provide encouragement and accountability throughout the process.

The detailed examples and case studies presented in this chapter illustrate the application of strategies for building healthy habits in real-life scenarios. They highlight the potential for significant improvement and recovery when individuals actively engage in the process and utilize the strategies and tools discussed.

By incorporating these strategies into their lives, individuals can achieve meaningful and lasting recovery from compulsive behaviors. With the right tools, techniques, and support, it is possible to overcome the challenges posed by compulsive behaviors and work towards a healthier, more balanced future.

Chapter 9: The Power of Support Networks

Building a Strong Support System

A robust support system is essential for individuals seeking to overcome compulsive behaviors. It provides emotional, psychological, and practical assistance, fostering a sense of belonging and understanding. Building a strong support network involves identifying and engaging with individuals and groups who can offer various forms of support throughout the recovery process.

1. Identifying Potential Support Sources

- Family Members: Close family members, such as parents, siblings, and spouses, can provide continuous emotional and practical support. They often have a deep understanding of the individual's struggles and can offer a safe space for open communication.

- Friends: Trusted friends can offer companionship, empathy, and encouragement. They can help the individual stay engaged in social activities and provide a sense of normalcy and connection.

- Mental Health Professionals: Therapists, counselors, and psychiatrists play a critical role in providing professional guidance and treatment. They offer evidence-based interventions and support tailored to the individual's needs.

- Support Groups: Peer support groups provide a community of individuals who share similar experiences. These groups offer a platform for sharing, learning, and mutual encouragement.

- Online Communities: Online forums and social media groups can offer additional support, especially for those who may not have access to local resources. These communities provide a sense of belonging and can be a source of valuable information and encouragement.

2. Engaging with Support Sources

- Open Communication: Open and honest communication is vital when engaging with potential support sources. Share your struggles, goals, and needs with family, friends, and professionals. Transparency fosters understanding and builds trust.

- Setting Boundaries: Establish clear boundaries to ensure that support interactions are healthy and productive. Discuss what kind of support is helpful and what may be counterproductive.

- Seeking Professional Guidance: Engage with mental health professionals who specialize in treating compulsive behaviors. They can offer personalized treatment plans, monitor progress, and provide ongoing support.

- Joining Support Groups: Actively participate in support groups that focus on compulsive behaviors. Attend meetings regularly, share your experiences, and learn from others in similar situations.

3. Maintaining a Strong Support System

- Regular Check-ins: Maintain regular contact with your support network. Schedule check-ins with family, friends, and professionals to discuss progress, challenges, and goals.

- Expressing Gratitude: Show appreciation for the support you receive. Expressing gratitude strengthens relationships and fosters a positive support environment.

- Being Supportive in Return: Support is a two-way street. Offer support to others in your network, creating a reciprocal and mutually beneficial relationship.

The Role of Family and Friends in Recovery

FAMILY AND FRIENDS play a crucial role in the recovery process from compulsive behaviors. Their support can significantly impact an individual's motivation, resilience, and overall well-being. Understanding the specific ways in which family and friends can contribute to recovery is essential for building an effective support system.

1. Emotional Support

- Listening and Empathy: One of the most valuable forms of support is simply being there to listen. Providing a non-judgmental, empathetic ear can help the individual feel understood and less isolated.

- Encouragement: Offer words of encouragement and affirmation. Positive reinforcement can boost the individual's confidence and motivation to stay committed to their recovery goals.

2. Practical Support

- Assistance with Daily Tasks: Compulsive behaviors can interfere with daily functioning. Offering help with tasks such as household chores, running errands, or managing appointments can reduce stress and allow the individual to focus on recovery.

- Creating a Structured Environment: Help establish a structured and supportive environment that minimizes triggers and promotes healthy routines. This may include organizing living spaces, creating schedules, and encouraging healthy habits.

3. Accountability

- Monitoring Progress: Act as an accountability partner by monitoring the individual's progress and providing gentle reminders of their goals. This can help the individual stay on track and recognize their achievements.

- Setting Boundaries: Establish and enforce healthy boundaries to prevent enabling compulsive behaviors. Encourage responsible behavior and support the individual's efforts to make positive changes.

4. Educational Support

- Learning About the Condition: Educate yourself about compulsive behaviors and their treatment. Understanding the condition can help you provide informed support and reduce misconceptions or stigma.

- Encouraging Professional Help: Encourage the individual to seek professional help and adhere to their treatment plan. Support their attendance at therapy sessions and other appointments.

5. Social Support

- Maintaining Social Connections: Help the individual maintain social connections and engage in activities that bring joy and fulfillment. Social interactions can provide a sense of normalcy and reduce feelings of isolation.

- Participating in Activities: Join the individual in activities that promote well-being, such as exercise, hobbies, or mindfulness practices. Participating together can strengthen your bond and provide mutual support.

Joining and Benefiting from Support Groups

SUPPORT GROUPS OFFER a unique and valuable form of support for individuals recovering from compulsive behaviors. They provide a sense of community, shared understanding, and mutual encouragement. Joining and actively participating in support groups can significantly enhance the recovery process.

1. Types of Support Groups

- Peer-Led Groups: These groups are typically led by individuals who have experienced similar challenges. Peer-led groups offer a sense of camaraderie and shared understanding.

- Professionally-Led Groups: These groups are facilitated by mental health professionals who provide structured support and guidance. Professionally-led groups often include therapeutic interventions and education.

- Online Support Groups: Online groups offer flexibility and accessibility for individuals who may not have access to local resources. These groups can be found on social media platforms, forums, and specialized websites.

2. Finding the Right Support Group

- Research: Research various support groups to find one that aligns with your needs and preferences. Consider factors such as the group's focus, size, format (in-person or online), and facilitator.

- Trial and Error: It may take some trial and error to find the right fit. Attend a few different groups to see which one feels most supportive and beneficial.

- Seeking Recommendations: Ask your therapist, healthcare provider, or trusted individuals for recommendations on reputable support groups.

3. Participating in Support Groups

- Regular Attendance: Commit to attending meetings regularly. Consistent participation helps build relationships, gain insights, and receive ongoing support.

- Active Engagement: Actively engage in group discussions, share your experiences, and listen to others. Open and honest communication fosters a supportive and collaborative environment.

- Confidentiality: Respect the confidentiality of group members. Creating a safe and trusting space is essential for meaningful support.

4. Benefits of Support Groups

- Shared Understanding: Being part of a group of individuals who share similar experiences can reduce feelings of isolation and provide a sense of belonging.

- Emotional Support: Support groups offer a platform for expressing emotions, receiving validation, and providing mutual encouragement.

- Practical Advice: Group members often share practical advice, coping strategies, and resources that can be helpful in managing compulsive behaviors.

- Accountability: The group setting provides accountability, encouraging members to stay committed to their recovery goals.

- Inspiration and Motivation: Hearing success stories and witnessing the progress of others can inspire and motivate individuals to continue working towards their recovery.

Detailed Examples and Case Studies

TO ILLUSTRATE THE POWER of support networks, let's explore detailed examples and case studies of individuals who have benefited from building strong support systems, the role of family and friends in their recovery, and their experiences with support groups.

Case Study 1: Building a Strong Support System for Overcoming OCD

BACKGROUND: SARAH IS a 30-year-old woman who has been struggling with obsessive-compulsive disorder (OCD) for many years. Her compulsions include excessive handwashing and checking behaviors, which significantly interfere with her daily life and responsibilities.

Building a Strong Support System:

1. FAMILY SUPPORT:

- Open Communication: Sarah's family, including her parents and siblings, engaged in open and honest communication about her condition. They educated themselves about OCD and expressed their willingness to support her.

- Practical Assistance: Sarah's family helped her establish a structured routine, including designated times for handwashing and checking, to reduce the frequency of her compulsions. They also assisted with household chores and other responsibilities to reduce her stress.

2. Friends' Support:

- Companionship: Sarah's close friends provided companionship and emotional support. They spent time with her, engaging in activities she enjoyed, which helped distract her from her compulsions.

- Encouragement: Sarah's friends offered words of encouragement and affirmation, boosting her confidence and motivation to stay committed to her recovery goals.

3. Professional Support:

- Therapy: Sarah sought help from a therapist specializing in OCD. The therapist provided cognitive-behavioral therapy (CBT) and exposure and response prevention (ERP) techniques to help her manage her compulsions.

- Medication: Sarah's psychiatrist prescribed medication to help reduce her anxiety and OCD symptoms. Regular follow-up appointments ensured that her treatment plan was effective and adjusted as needed.

4. Support Groups:

- Joining a Support Group: Sarah joined a local support group for individuals with OCD. The group met weekly and provided a safe space for members to share their experiences, challenges, and successes.

- Online Communities: Sarah also participated in online forums and social media groups focused on OCD. These communities offered additional support and resources, especially during times when in-person meetings were not possible.

Outcome: With the support of her family, friends, professionals, and support groups, Sarah made significant progress in managing her OCD symptoms. The combination of practical assistance, emotional support, and professional treatment helped her reduce the frequency and intensity of her compulsions. Sarah continued to actively engage with her support network, maintaining her progress and working towards long-term recovery.

Case Study 2: The Role of Family and Friends in Recovery from Compulsive Hoarding

BACKGROUND: MARK IS a 50-year-old man who has been struggling with compulsive hoarding for over a decade. His home is filled with items he cannot bring himself to discard, including old newspapers, clothing, and broken appliances. The clutter has reached a point where most rooms are unusable, and his living conditions are hazardous.

The Role of Family and Friends:

1. FAMILY SUPPORT:

- Understanding and Empathy: Mark's family, including his wife and adult children, educated themselves about compulsive hoarding. They approached him with empathy and understanding, avoiding judgment or criticism.

- Practical Assistance: Mark's family helped him develop a plan to declutter his home gradually. They assisted with sorting through items, identifying what to keep, donate, or discard. They also helped organize the remaining items to create a safer and more functional living space.

2. Friends' Support:

- Emotional Support: Mark's close friends provided emotional support and encouragement. They listened to his concerns and offered reassurance during challenging times.

- Social Engagement: Mark's friends encouraged him to engage in social activities and hobbies that he enjoyed. These activities provided a positive distraction from his hoarding behaviors and helped improve his overall well-being.

3. Professional Support:

- Therapy: Mark sought help from a therapist specializing in hoarding disorder. The therapist provided cognitive-behavioral therapy (CBT) and motivational interviewing techniques to help him address the underlying causes of his hoarding behaviors.

- Medication: Mark's psychiatrist prescribed medication to help manage his anxiety and improve his ability to make decisions about his belongings. Regular follow-up appointments ensured that his treatment plan was effective and adjusted as needed.

4. Support Groups:

- Joining a Support Group: Mark joined a local support group for individuals with hoarding disorder. The group met bi-weekly and provided a platform for members to share their experiences, challenges, and successes.

- Online Communities: Mark also participated in online forums and social media groups focused on hoarding disorder. These communities offered additional support and resources, especially during times when in-person meetings were not possible.

Outcome: With the support of his family, friends, professionals, and support groups, Mark made significant progress in managing his compulsive hoarding behaviors. The combination of practical assistance, emotional support, and professional treatment helped him declutter his home and improve his living conditions. Mark continued to actively engage with his support network, maintaining his progress and working towards long-term recovery.

Case Study 3: Joining and Benefiting from Support Groups for Compulsive Gambling

BACKGROUND: EMILY IS a 40-year-old woman who has been struggling with compulsive gambling for many years. Her gambling behaviors have led to financial problems, strained relationships, and emotional distress.

Joining and Benefiting from Support Groups:

1. FINDING THE RIGHT Support Group:

- Research: Emily researched various support groups for compulsive gambling and found a local Gamblers Anonymous (GA) group that met weekly.

- Trial and Error: Emily attended a few different support groups to find the right fit. She chose the GA group that felt most supportive and beneficial.

2. Participating in Support Groups:

- Regular Attendance: Emily committed to attending the GA meetings regularly. Consistent participation helped her build relationships, gain insights, and receive ongoing support.

- Active Engagement: Emily actively engaged in group discussions, sharing her experiences and listening to others. Open and honest communication fostered a supportive and collaborative environment.

- Confidentiality: Emily respected the confidentiality of group members, creating a safe and trusting space for meaningful support.

3. Benefits of Support Groups:

- Shared Understanding: Being part of a group of individuals who shared similar experiences reduced Emily's feelings of isolation and provided a sense of belonging.

- Emotional Support: The GA group offered a platform for expressing emotions, receiving validation, and providing mutual encouragement.

- Practical Advice: Group members shared practical advice, coping strategies, and resources that helped Emily manage her gambling behaviors.

- Accountability: The group setting provided accountability, encouraging Emily to stay committed to her recovery goals.

- Inspiration and Motivation: Hearing success stories and witnessing the progress of others inspired and motivated Emily to continue working towards her recovery.

4. Online Support Groups:

- Flexibility and Accessibility: Emily also joined online support groups for compulsive gambling. These groups offered flexibility and accessibility, allowing her to receive support even when she couldn't attend in-person meetings.

- Additional Resources: Online groups provided valuable information and resources, including articles, videos, and discussion forums.

Outcome: With the support of her GA group, online communities, and professional guidance, Emily made significant progress in managing her compulsive gambling behaviors. The combination of shared understanding, emotional support, practical advice, and accountability helped her reduce her gambling activities and improve her financial and emotional well-being. Emily continued to actively participate in her support groups, maintaining her progress and working towards long-term recovery.

Conclusion

The power of support networks cannot be overstated in the journey towards recovery from compulsive behaviors. Building a strong support system, involving family, friends, professionals, and support groups, provides a comprehensive and multifaceted approach to overcoming these challenges.

Family and friends play a crucial role in providing emotional, practical, and social support. Their understanding, empathy, and encouragement can significantly impact an individual's motivation, resilience, and overall well-being. Engaging with mental health professionals ensures access to evidence-based treatments and expert guidance.

Support groups offer a unique and valuable form of support, providing a sense of community, shared understanding, and mutual encouragement. Joining and actively participating in support groups can significantly enhance the recovery process by offering emotional support, practical advice, accountability, and inspiration.

The detailed examples and case studies presented in this chapter illustrate the power of support networks in real-life scenarios. They highlight the potential for significant improvement and recovery when individuals actively engage with their support networks and utilize the resources and support available to them.

By building and maintaining strong support networks, individuals can achieve meaningful and lasting recovery from compulsive behaviors. With the right tools, techniques, and support, it is possible to overcome the challenges posed by compulsive behaviors and work towards a healthier, more balanced future.

Chapter 10: Dealing with Relapse

Understanding Relapse and Its Triggers

Relapse is a common part of the recovery process for many individuals struggling with compulsive behaviors. Understanding relapse, its triggers, and how to manage it is crucial for long-term success. Relapse is not a sign of failure but rather an opportunity to learn and strengthen one's recovery strategies.

1. Defining Relapse

- Relapse: A relapse occurs when an individual returns to their compulsive behaviors after a period of improvement. This can be a full return to old patterns or a slip, which is a brief return to the behavior.

- Slip vs. Relapse: It's important to distinguish between a slip and a full relapse. A slip is a single instance or a brief period of returning to compulsive behavior, while a relapse is a sustained return to old patterns.

2. Common Triggers for Relapse

- Stress: High levels of stress, whether due to work, relationships, or other factors, can trigger a relapse. Stress can increase anxiety and emotional distress, leading individuals to return to compulsive behaviors as a coping mechanism.

- Emotional Distress: Negative emotions such as sadness, anger, loneliness, and frustration can trigger a relapse. These emotions can create a sense of overwhelm, prompting individuals to seek relief through their compulsive behaviors.

- Environmental Cues: Certain environments or situations associated with past compulsive behaviors can act as triggers. This might include specific places, people, or activities that remind the individual of their compulsions.

- Social Pressure: Peer pressure or social situations where others are engaging in similar behaviors can trigger a relapse. This is particularly relevant for behaviors like substance abuse or gambling.

- Overconfidence: Feeling overly confident about one's ability to manage compulsive behaviors can lead to complacency. This overconfidence might cause individuals to let down their guard, making them more vulnerable to relapse.

- Lack of Support: A weak or nonexistent support network can increase the risk of relapse. Support from family, friends, and professionals provides accountability, encouragement, and guidance, which are essential for maintaining recovery.

3. Signs of Impending Relapse

- Increased Cravings or Urges: A noticeable increase in cravings or urges to engage in the compulsive behavior can be a sign of impending relapse.

- Isolation: Withdrawing from social activities or support networks can indicate that an individual is struggling and at risk of relapse.

- Negative Thinking: A return to negative thought patterns, such as self-criticism, hopelessness, or rationalizing the compulsive behavior, can signal an impending relapse.

- Decreased Self-Care: Neglecting self-care routines, such as exercise, healthy eating, or sleep, can increase vulnerability to relapse.

- Engaging in Risky Situations: Placing oneself in environments or situations that trigger the compulsive behavior can increase the risk of relapse.

Strategies for Preventing and Managing Relapse

PREVENTING AND MANAGING relapse involves developing a comprehensive plan that includes identifying triggers, building resilience, and implementing practical strategies. A proactive approach can help individuals navigate challenges and maintain their recovery.

1. Identifying Triggers and Creating a Plan

- Trigger Identification: Regularly review and update the list of triggers that might lead to a relapse. Awareness of these triggers allows for better preparation and response.

- Developing a Relapse Prevention Plan: Create a detailed plan outlining specific strategies for managing triggers and preventing relapse. This plan should include coping mechanisms, support contacts, and emergency steps to take if a relapse occurs.

2. Building Resilience

- Stress Management: Develop and practice stress management techniques such as mindfulness, meditation, deep breathing exercises, and progressive muscle relaxation. These techniques can help reduce the impact of stress and prevent relapse.

- Emotional Regulation: Enhance emotional regulation skills through therapies such as cognitive-behavioral therapy (CBT) or dialectical behavior therapy (DBT). Learning to manage negative emotions constructively reduces the risk of relapse.

- Healthy Lifestyle: Maintain a healthy lifestyle that includes regular exercise, a balanced diet, adequate sleep, and regular self-care. A healthy body and mind are more resilient to stress and less prone to relapse.

- Support Network: Strengthen and maintain a robust support network. Regular contact with supportive family, friends, and professionals provides a safety net and encourages accountability.

3. Practical Strategies for Managing Triggers

- Avoidance: When possible, avoid situations or environments that are known triggers for compulsive behaviors. If avoidance is not possible, plan ahead on how to handle the situation.

- Alternative Activities: Engage in alternative activities that provide a positive outlet and distraction from compulsive behaviors. Hobbies, creative pursuits, and social activities can help fill the void left by the compulsive behavior.

- Mindfulness and Grounding Techniques: Practice mindfulness and grounding techniques to stay present and manage cravings. Techniques such as body scanning, mindful breathing, and grounding exercises can reduce the intensity of cravings.

- Cognitive Restructuring: Use cognitive restructuring techniques to challenge and reframe negative thought patterns. Identifying irrational thoughts and replacing them with balanced, realistic thoughts can reduce the likelihood of relapse.

4. Developing a Crisis Plan

- Emergency Contacts: Create a list of emergency contacts, including therapists, support group members, and trusted friends or family. Having a readily available list ensures quick access to support when needed.

- Immediate Actions: Outline immediate actions to take if a relapse occurs. This might include contacting a support person, using a specific coping mechanism, or removing oneself from the triggering environment.

- Post-Relapse Steps: Plan steps to take after a relapse to get back on track. This might include scheduling an extra therapy session, attending a support group meeting, or revisiting the relapse prevention plan.

Learning from Setbacks and Moving Forward

SETBACKS AND RELAPSES are not failures but opportunities for growth and learning. Understanding how to learn from these experiences and move forward is essential for long-term recovery.

1. Reflecting on the Relapse

- Objective Analysis: Reflect on the relapse without judgment. Analyze the circumstances, triggers, and emotions that led to the relapse. Understanding these factors provides valuable insights for future prevention.

- Identifying Gaps: Identify any gaps in the relapse prevention plan or coping strategies. Determine what worked well and what needs improvement.

2. Learning and Adapting

- Adjusting Strategies: Based on the analysis, adjust and strengthen the relapse prevention plan. Incorporate new strategies or modify existing ones to better address the identified triggers.

- Building New Skills: Use the relapse as an opportunity to build new skills. This might include learning new coping mechanisms, enhancing emotional regulation, or developing better stress management techniques.

3. Seeking Support and Guidance

- Professional Help: Seek additional support from therapists or counselors. Professional guidance can provide new perspectives, tools, and encouragement.

- Support Groups: Reconnect with support groups or consider joining new ones. Sharing experiences and learning from others can reinforce commitment to recovery.

4. Reaffirming Commitment to Recovery

- Setting New Goals: Set new, realistic goals for recovery. These goals should be specific, measurable, and achievable.

- Positive Self-Talk: Practice positive self-talk and self-compassion. Remind yourself that relapse is part of the recovery journey and that you have the strength and resilience to move forward.

5. Celebrating Progress

- Acknowledging Achievements: Celebrate your progress and achievements, no matter how small. Recognize the effort and dedication you have put into your recovery.

- Rewarding Yourself: Set up a reward system for achieving milestones. Rewards can be small treats, activities you enjoy, or other incentives that motivate you to stay on track.

Detailed Examples and Case Studies

TO ILLUSTRATE HOW TO deal with relapse effectively, let's explore detailed examples and case studies of individuals who have experienced relapse, learned from their setbacks, and successfully moved forward in their recovery.

Case Study 1: Managing Relapse in Compulsive Eating

BACKGROUND: EMILY IS a 35-year-old woman who has been struggling with compulsive eating for several years. She made significant progress in managing her behavior through therapy, mindful eating practices, and a healthy lifestyle. However, a stressful period at work triggered a relapse.

Understanding the Relapse:

1. TRIGGER IDENTIFICATION: Emily identified that increased work stress, coupled with feelings of inadequacy and loneliness, triggered her relapse. She found herself returning to old patterns of using food for comfort.

2. Signs of Impending Relapse: Emily noticed increased cravings, negative self-talk, and a tendency to isolate herself from her support network.

Strategies for Managing Relapse:

1. REFLECTING ON THE Relapse:

- Objective Analysis: Emily reflected on the relapse without judgment. She acknowledged the triggers and emotions involved and identified gaps in her coping strategies.

- Identifying Gaps: Emily realized that she had neglected her self-care routines and had not communicated her struggles to her support network.

2. Learning and Adapting:

- Adjusting Strategies: Emily adjusted her relapse prevention plan to include additional stress management techniques, such as regular mindfulness meditation and journaling.

- Building New Skills: Emily worked with her therapist to develop new coping mechanisms, such as using exercise and creative outlets to manage stress.

3. Seeking Support and Guidance:

- Professional Help: Emily scheduled extra therapy sessions to work through her emotions and reinforce her commitment to recovery.

- Support Groups: Emily reconnected with her support group for compulsive eating, sharing her experience and receiving encouragement and advice from others.

4. Reaffirming Commitment to Recovery:

- Setting New Goals: Emily set new, realistic goals for her recovery, including maintaining a balanced diet, practicing mindful eating, and engaging in regular physical activity.

- Positive Self-Talk: Emily practiced positive self-talk, reminding herself of her progress and strength. She embraced self-compassion, understanding that relapse is part of the recovery journey.

5. Celebrating Progress:

- Acknowledging Achievements: Emily acknowledged her achievements, such as successfully navigating a stressful work period without returning to compulsive eating.

- Rewarding Yourself: Emily rewarded herself with non-food treats, such as a spa day or a weekend getaway, to celebrate her progress and reinforce her commitment to recovery.

Outcome: Emily successfully managed her relapse and used the experience to strengthen her recovery strategies. She continued to actively engage with her support network, maintain her healthy lifestyle, and build resilience against future triggers.

Case Study 2: Preventing Relapse in Compulsive Shopping

BACKGROUND: MARK IS a 40-year-old man who has been struggling with compulsive shopping for many years. He made significant progress in managing his behavior through therapy, financial planning, and mindfulness practices. However, a holiday season with increased social pressure triggered a relapse.

Understanding the Relapse:

1. TRIGGER IDENTIFICATION: Mark identified that social pressure and the holiday season's emphasis on spending triggered his relapse. He found himself returning to old patterns of buying unnecessary items to cope with stress and fit in socially.

2. Signs of Impending Relapse: Mark noticed increased cravings to shop, rationalizing unnecessary purchases, and a decline in his financial planning efforts.

Strategies for Managing Relapse:

1. REFLECTING ON THE Relapse:

- Objective Analysis: Mark reflected on the relapse without judgment. He acknowledged the triggers and emotions involved and identified gaps in his coping strategies.

- Identifying Gaps: Mark realized that he had neglected his financial planning routines and had not communicated his struggles to his support network.

2. Learning and Adapting:

- Adjusting Strategies: Mark adjusted his relapse prevention plan to include additional financial planning techniques, such as setting strict budgets and using cash-only transactions during the holiday season.

- Building New Skills: Mark worked with his therapist to develop new coping mechanisms, such as using mindfulness meditation and social activities that did not involve shopping.

3. Seeking Support and Guidance:

- Professional Help: Mark scheduled extra therapy sessions to work through his emotions and reinforce his commitment to recovery.

- Support Groups: Mark reconnected with his support group for compulsive shopping, sharing his experience and receiving encouragement and advice from others.

4. Reaffirming Commitment to Recovery:

- Setting New Goals: Mark set new, realistic goals for his recovery, including maintaining a strict budget, avoiding shopping malls, and engaging in alternative social activities.

- Positive Self-Talk: Mark practiced positive self-talk, reminding himself of his progress and strength. He embraced self-compassion, understanding that relapse is part of the recovery journey.

5. Celebrating Progress:

- Acknowledging Achievements: Mark acknowledged his achievements, such as successfully navigating the holiday season without returning to compulsive shopping.

- Rewarding Yourself: Mark rewarded himself with non-shopping treats, such as a special dinner or a new hobby-related item, to celebrate his progress and reinforce his commitment to recovery.

Outcome: Mark successfully managed his relapse and used the experience to strengthen his recovery strategies. He continued to actively engage with his support network, maintain his financial planning routines, and build resilience against future triggers.

Case Study 3: Managing Relapse in Substance Abuse

BACKGROUND: SARAH IS a 28-year-old woman who has been struggling with substance abuse for several years. She made significant progress in managing her behavior through therapy, support groups, and a healthy lifestyle. However, a family conflict triggered a relapse.

Understanding the Relapse:

1. TRIGGER IDENTIFICATION: Sarah identified that a heated family conflict, coupled with feelings of anger and betrayal, triggered her relapse. She found herself returning to old patterns of using substances to cope with her emotions.

2. Signs of Impending Relapse: Sarah noticed increased cravings for substances, negative self-talk, and a tendency to isolate herself from her support network.

Strategies for Managing Relapse:

1. REFLECTING ON THE Relapse:

- Objective Analysis: Sarah reflected on the relapse without judgment. She acknowledged the triggers and emotions involved and identified gaps in her coping strategies.

- Identifying Gaps: Sarah realized that she had not communicated her struggles to her support network and had neglected her emotional regulation routines.

2. Learning and Adapting:

- Adjusting Strategies: Sarah adjusted her relapse prevention plan to include additional emotional regulation techniques, such as regular mindfulness meditation and journaling.

- Building New Skills: Sarah worked with her therapist to develop new coping mechanisms, such as using exercise and creative outlets to manage her emotions.

3. Seeking Support and Guidance:

- Professional Help: Sarah scheduled extra therapy sessions to work through her emotions and reinforce her commitment to recovery.

- Support Groups: Sarah reconnected with her support group for substance abuse, sharing her experience and receiving encouragement and advice from others.

4. Reaffirming Commitment to Recovery:

- Setting New Goals: Sarah set new, realistic goals for her recovery, including maintaining a healthy lifestyle, practicing emotional regulation, and engaging in regular social activities.

- Positive Self-Talk: Sarah practiced positive self-talk, reminding herself of her progress and strength. She embraced self-compassion, understanding that relapse is part of the recovery journey.

5. Celebrating Progress:

- Acknowledging Achievements: Sarah acknowledged her achievements, such as successfully navigating the family conflict without returning to substance abuse.

- Rewarding Yourself: Sarah rewarded herself with non-substance-related treats, such as a spa day or a weekend getaway, to celebrate her progress and reinforce her commitment to recovery.

Outcome: Sarah successfully managed her relapse and used the experience to strengthen her recovery strategies. She continued to actively engage with her support network, maintain her healthy lifestyle, and build resilience against future triggers.

Conclusion

Dealing with relapse is an integral part of the recovery journey from compulsive behaviors. Understanding relapse, its triggers, and how to manage it effectively is crucial for long-term success. Relapse is not a sign of failure but an opportunity to learn and strengthen one's recovery strategies.

Identifying triggers, building resilience, and implementing practical strategies for preventing and managing relapse can help individuals navigate challenges and maintain their recovery. Developing a crisis plan and seeking support and guidance from professionals and support groups are essential steps in managing relapse.

Learning from setbacks and moving forward involves reflecting on the relapse, adjusting strategies, and reaffirming commitment to recovery. Celebrating progress and practicing self-compassion are vital components of the recovery process.

The detailed examples and case studies presented in this chapter illustrate how individuals can effectively manage relapse, learn from their setbacks, and move forward in their recovery journey. By incorporating these strategies and tools into their lives, individuals can achieve meaningful and lasting recovery from compulsive behaviors. With the right support, resilience, and determination, it is possible to overcome the challenges posed by relapse and work towards a healthier, more balanced future.

Chapter 11: Nutrition and Exercise

The Impact of Diet and Physical Activity on Mental Health

The connection between physical health and mental health is profound and multifaceted. Proper nutrition and regular exercise play critical roles in maintaining mental well-being and mitigating the symptoms of various mental health conditions, including compulsive behaviors.

1. The Interplay Between Diet and Mental Health

- Nutrient Intake and Brain Function: The brain requires a variety of nutrients to function optimally. Deficiencies in essential nutrients can impair brain function and contribute to mental health issues.

- Gut-Brain Axis: The gut and brain are connected through a complex network known as the gut-brain axis. The health of the gut microbiome significantly affects mental health, influencing mood, cognition, and overall well-being.

- Inflammation and Mental Health: Chronic inflammation is linked to various mental health disorders. Certain diets can reduce inflammation and thus potentially improve mental health outcomes.

2. The Role of Physical Activity in Mental Health

- Neurochemical Changes: Exercise induces changes in brain chemistry, including the release of endorphins and neurotransmitters such as serotonin and dopamine, which elevate mood and reduce symptoms of depression and anxiety.

- Cognitive Function: Regular physical activity enhances cognitive function, improving memory, attention, and executive function. It also promotes neurogenesis, the creation of new neurons, which is beneficial for overall brain health.

- Stress Reduction: Exercise is a powerful stress reliever. Physical activity helps lower cortisol levels and reduces the physiological impacts of stress on the body.

Nutritional Tips for Supporting Brain Health

A WELL-BALANCED DIET rich in essential nutrients can support brain health, improve mood, and enhance cognitive function. Here are some nutritional tips to help support mental well-being.

1. Essential Nutrients for Brain Health

- Omega-3 Fatty Acids: Omega-3 fatty acids, found in fatty fish (such as salmon and mackerel), flaxseeds, chia seeds, and walnuts, are crucial for brain health. They play a role in building cell membranes in the brain and have anti-inflammatory effects.

- B Vitamins: B vitamins, including B6, B12, and folic acid, are essential for brain function. They are involved in the production of neurotransmitters and can reduce the risk of cognitive decline. Good sources include leafy greens, legumes, eggs, and meat.

- Antioxidants: Antioxidants protect the brain from oxidative stress and inflammation. Foods rich in antioxidants include berries (blueberries, strawberries), dark chocolate, nuts, seeds, and vegetables (spinach, kale).

- Magnesium: Magnesium is important for brain function and can help reduce anxiety and stress. Sources of magnesium include nuts, seeds, whole grains, and leafy green vegetables.

- Vitamin D: Vitamin D is linked to mood regulation and cognitive function. Sun exposure is a natural source, and it can also be found in fatty fish, fortified dairy products, and supplements if necessary.

2. Dietary Patterns for Mental Health

- Mediterranean Diet: The Mediterranean diet, rich in fruits, vegetables, whole grains, nuts, seeds, and healthy fats (such as olive oil), has been associated with reduced risks of depression and cognitive decline. It emphasizes natural, unprocessed foods and limits red meat and refined sugars.

- Anti-Inflammatory Diet: An anti-inflammatory diet includes foods that reduce inflammation, such as leafy greens, fatty fish, nuts, and seeds. It avoids pro-inflammatory foods like processed foods, refined sugars, and trans fats.

- Plant-Based Diet: A plant-based diet, which focuses on vegetables, fruits, legumes, nuts, and seeds, can support brain health by providing essential nutrients and reducing inflammation. However, it's important to ensure adequate intake of nutrients that are less abundant in plant-based foods, such as B12 and omega-3 fatty acids.

3. Tips for Healthy Eating Habits

- Balanced Meals: Aim for balanced meals that include a mix of protein, healthy fats, and complex carbohydrates. This balance helps stabilize blood sugar levels, which can affect mood and energy.

- Regular Meal Times: Eating regular meals can prevent blood sugar spikes and crashes, which can impact mood and cognitive function. Avoid skipping meals, as this can lead to irritability and decreased concentration.

- Hydration: Staying hydrated is crucial for brain function. Dehydration can impair cognitive function and mood. Aim to drink at least eight glasses of water a day.

- Mindful Eating: Practice mindful eating by paying attention to what you eat, savoring each bite, and listening to your body's hunger and fullness cues. This can help prevent overeating and improve digestion.

Exercise Routines to Reduce Stress and Improve Mood

REGULAR PHYSICAL ACTIVITY is one of the most effective ways to reduce stress and improve mood. Here are some exercise routines and practices that can help enhance mental well-being.

1. Aerobic Exercise

- Overview: Aerobic exercise, also known as cardio, includes activities that increase your heart rate and breathing. Examples include walking, running, cycling, and swimming.

- Benefits: Aerobic exercise increases the release of endorphins, which are natural mood lifters. It also helps reduce anxiety, depression, and stress, and improves overall cardiovascular health.

- Routine: Aim for at least 150 minutes of moderate-intensity aerobic exercise per week, or 75 minutes of vigorous-intensity exercise. This can be broken down into 30-minute sessions, five days a week.

2. Strength Training

- Overview: Strength training involves exercises that build muscle mass and strength, such as lifting weights, resistance band exercises, and bodyweight exercises (e.g., push-ups, squats).

- Benefits: Strength training improves muscle strength, bone density, and metabolic rate. It also enhances mood and self-esteem, and can help reduce symptoms of depression and anxiety.

- Routine: Aim to incorporate strength training exercises into your routine at least two days a week. Focus on major muscle groups, performing 8-12 repetitions of each exercise.

3. Yoga and Pilates

- Overview: Yoga and Pilates are mind-body exercises that combine physical movement with breath control and mindfulness. They include poses and sequences that enhance flexibility, strength, and relaxation.

- Benefits: These practices reduce stress, improve flexibility and strength, and promote relaxation. They also enhance mindfulness, which can help manage anxiety and improve mood.

- Routine: Practice yoga or Pilates 2-3 times a week. There are many styles and levels to choose from, so find a practice that suits your preferences and abilities.

4. High-Intensity Interval Training (HIIT)

- Overview: HIIT involves short bursts of intense exercise followed by brief periods of rest or low-intensity exercise. Examples include sprints, jumping jacks, and burpees.

- Benefits: HIIT can improve cardiovascular fitness, burn calories, and boost metabolism in a shorter amount of time compared to traditional workouts. It also increases the release of endorphins and other mood-enhancing chemicals.

- Routine: Incorporate HIIT sessions into your routine 1-2 times a week. Each session can last between 20-30 minutes, with exercises performed at high intensity for 30-60 seconds followed by rest periods.

5. Mindfulness and Relaxation Exercises

- Overview: Mindfulness and relaxation exercises include practices such as deep breathing, progressive muscle relaxation, and guided imagery.

- Benefits: These exercises reduce stress and anxiety, promote relaxation, and improve sleep quality. They also enhance self-awareness and emotional regulation.

- Routine: Practice mindfulness and relaxation exercises daily or as needed. Even a few minutes of focused breathing or relaxation can have significant benefits for mental well-being.

Detailed Examples and Case Studies

TO ILLUSTRATE THE IMPACT of nutrition and exercise on mental health, let's explore detailed examples and case studies of individuals who have successfully improved their mental well-being through dietary changes and physical activity.

Case Study 1: Improving Mental Health Through a Balanced Diet

BACKGROUND: JANE IS a 32-year-old woman who has been struggling with anxiety and depression for several years. She often experiences low energy, poor concentration, and mood swings.

Nutritional Changes:

1. CONSULTING A NUTRITIONIST: Jane consulted a nutritionist to evaluate her diet and identify areas for improvement. The nutritionist recommended incorporating more whole foods and essential nutrients into her diet.

2. Increasing Omega-3 Intake: Jane added more sources of omega-3 fatty acids to her diet, including fatty fish, flaxseeds, and walnuts. These changes helped improve her mood and cognitive function.

3. Incorporating Antioxidants: Jane increased her intake of antioxidant-rich foods, such as berries, dark chocolate, and leafy greens. This helped reduce inflammation and improve her overall brain health.

4. Balancing Meals: Jane focused on creating balanced meals that included a mix of protein, healthy fats, and complex carbohydrates. She also established regular meal times to stabilize her blood sugar levels.

Outcome: Over several months, Jane experienced significant improvements in her mental health. Her energy levels increased, her mood stabilized, and her concentration improved. The combination of a balanced diet rich in essential nutrients helped support her overall well-being.

Case Study 2: Reducing Stress and Anxiety Through Exercise

BACKGROUND: MARK IS a 45-year-old man who has been struggling with high levels of stress and anxiety due to his demanding job. He often feels overwhelmed and finds it difficult to relax.

Exercise Routine:

1. AEROBIC EXERCISE: Mark started incorporating aerobic exercise into his routine by going for a 30-minute run three times a week. This helped him release endorphins and reduce his anxiety levels.

2. Strength Training: Mark added strength training exercises, such as weightlifting and resistance band exercises, to his routine twice a week. This improved his physical strength and boosted his self-esteem.

3. Yoga: Mark began practicing yoga twice a week to enhance his flexibility and promote relaxation. The mindfulness and breath control aspects of yoga helped him manage his stress more effectively.

4. HIIT: Mark included a 20-minute HIIT session once a week to improve his cardiovascular fitness and boost his metabolism. The intense bursts of exercise helped him release built-up stress and tension.

Outcome: Over several months, Mark experienced significant reductions in his stress and anxiety levels. He felt more relaxed, focused, and in control of his emotions. The combination of aerobic exercise, strength training, yoga, and HIIT helped improve his overall mental well-being.

Case Study 3: Enhancing Cognitive Function Through Diet and Exercise

BACKGROUND: SARAH IS a 28-year-old woman who has been struggling with brain fog and difficulty concentrating. She often feels mentally fatigued and finds it challenging to stay focused.

Nutritional and Exercise Changes:

1. OMEGA-3 FATTY ACIDS: Sarah increased her intake of omega-3 fatty acids by eating more fatty fish, chia seeds, and flaxseeds. This helped improve her cognitive function and reduce brain fog.

2. B Vitamins: Sarah incorporated more B vitamin-rich foods, such as leafy greens, eggs, and legumes, into her diet. This supported her brain health and enhanced her cognitive abilities.

3. Regular Exercise: Sarah started a regular exercise routine that included a mix of aerobic exercise, strength training, and yoga. She exercised for at least 30 minutes, five days a week.

4. Mindfulness and Relaxation: Sarah practiced mindfulness meditation and deep breathing exercises daily to reduce stress and improve her focus. These practices helped her stay present and manage mental fatigue.

Outcome: Over several months, Sarah experienced significant improvements in her cognitive function. Her brain fog lifted, and she found it easier to concentrate and stay focused. The combination of a nutrient-rich diet and regular exercise helped enhance her mental clarity and overall well-being.

Conclusion

The impact of nutrition and exercise on mental health is profound and multifaceted. Proper nutrition and regular physical activity play critical roles in maintaining mental well-being and mitigating the symptoms of various mental health conditions, including compulsive behaviors.

A well-balanced diet rich in essential nutrients, such as omega-3 fatty acids, B vitamins, antioxidants, magnesium, and vitamin D, supports brain health, improves mood, and enhances cognitive function. Adopting dietary patterns such as the Mediterranean diet, anti-inflammatory diet, and plant-based diet can further support mental well-being.

Regular physical activity, including aerobic exercise, strength training, yoga, HIIT, and mindfulness practices, reduces stress, improves mood, and enhances cognitive function. Developing a consistent exercise routine and incorporating mindfulness and relaxation exercises into daily life can significantly improve mental health outcomes.

The detailed examples and case studies presented in this chapter illustrate how individuals can successfully improve their mental well-being through dietary changes and physical activity. By incorporating these strategies into their lives, individuals can achieve meaningful and lasting improvements in their mental health. With the right tools, techniques, and support, it is possible to overcome the challenges posed by mental health conditions and work towards a healthier, more balanced future.

Chapter 12: Holistic Approaches

Alternative Therapies: Acupuncture, Yoga, and Aromatherapy

Holistic approaches to health and wellness consider the whole person—mind, body, and spirit—in the quest for optimal well-being. Alternative therapies, including acupuncture, yoga, and aromatherapy, are integral components of holistic health care. These therapies can complement traditional medical treatments and offer additional avenues for managing compulsive behaviors and enhancing mental health.

1. Acupuncture

- Overview: Acupuncture is an ancient Chinese medical practice that involves inserting thin needles into specific points on the body to balance the flow of energy, or Qi, and promote healing.

- Mechanism: Acupuncture is believed to stimulate the central nervous system, releasing chemicals that alter the experience of pain and trigger the body's natural healing processes. It also influences neurotransmitter levels, which can affect mood and emotional well-being.

- ***Applications***:

- Pain Relief: Acupuncture is widely recognized for its effectiveness in treating chronic pain, including headaches, back pain, and arthritis.

- Mental Health: Acupuncture can help alleviate symptoms of anxiety, depression, and stress. It is often used as a complementary therapy for these conditions.

- Compulsive Behaviors: By promoting relaxation and reducing anxiety, acupuncture can help manage compulsive behaviors. It may also address underlying physical and emotional imbalances contributing to these behaviors.

2. Yoga

- Overview: Yoga is a mind-body practice that combines physical postures, breath control, and meditation to enhance physical, mental, and spiritual well-being. Originating in ancient India, yoga has been practiced for thousands of years.

- Mechanism: Yoga's physical postures (asanas) improve strength, flexibility, and balance. Breath control (pranayama) and meditation promote relaxation, reduce stress, and enhance mental clarity.

- Applications:

- Physical Health: Yoga improves overall physical fitness, flexibility, and strength. It can also help alleviate chronic pain and improve cardiovascular health.

- Mental Health: Regular yoga practice reduces stress, anxiety, and depression. It promotes emotional regulation and enhances mindfulness.

- Compulsive Behaviors: Yoga's emphasis on mindfulness and self-awareness can help individuals manage compulsive behaviors. It provides tools for coping with stress and anxiety, which are often triggers for these behaviors.

3. Aromatherapy

- Overview: Aromatherapy involves the use of essential oils extracted from plants to promote physical and emotional well-being. These oils are typically inhaled or applied to the skin.

- Mechanism: Essential oils can influence the brain's limbic system, which is involved in emotion and memory. This can lead to changes in mood and stress levels.

- Applications:

- Relaxation and Stress Relief: Essential oils like lavender, chamomile, and ylang-ylang are known for their calming effects and can help reduce stress and anxiety.

- Mood Enhancement: Oils such as citrus (orange, lemon) and peppermint can uplift mood and increase energy levels.

- Compulsive Behaviors: Aromatherapy can support the management of compulsive behaviors by promoting relaxation and reducing anxiety. It can be used as part of a daily self-care routine to create a calming environment.

Integrating Holistic Practices into a Comprehensive Treatment Plan

INTEGRATING HOLISTIC practices into a comprehensive treatment plan involves combining traditional medical treatments with alternative therapies to address all aspects of an individual's well-being. This approach can enhance the effectiveness of treatment and support long-term recovery from compulsive behaviors.

1. Assessment and Personalization

- Comprehensive Evaluation: Begin with a comprehensive evaluation by healthcare professionals to assess the individual's physical, mental, and emotional health. This evaluation should include a thorough medical history, current symptoms, and lifestyle factors.

- Personalized Plan: Develop a personalized treatment plan that incorporates both traditional medical treatments and holistic practices. The plan should be tailored to the individual's specific needs, preferences, and goals.

2. Combining Traditional and Holistic Treatments

- Medical Treatments: Continue with prescribed medications and conventional therapies (e.g., cognitive-behavioral therapy, counseling) as recommended by healthcare professionals.

- Holistic Practices: Integrate holistic practices such as acupuncture, yoga, and aromatherapy into the treatment plan. These practices can complement traditional treatments and provide additional benefits.

- Coordination of Care: Ensure that all healthcare providers involved in the treatment plan communicate and coordinate their efforts. This collaborative approach helps create a cohesive and effective treatment strategy.

3. Creating a Holistic Routine

- Daily Practices: Incorporate holistic practices into daily routines. This might include a morning yoga session, daily meditation, and the use of essential oils for relaxation.

- Self-Care: Emphasize the importance of self-care in maintaining overall well-being. Encourage practices such as regular exercise, healthy eating, adequate sleep, and mindfulness activities.

- Mind-Body Connection: Foster an awareness of the mind-body connection and how physical health impacts mental health. Encourage activities that promote this connection, such as mindful movement and breathwork.

4. Monitoring and Adjusting the Plan

- Regular Check-Ins: Schedule regular check-ins with healthcare providers to monitor progress and make any necessary adjustments to the treatment plan. These check-ins provide an opportunity to evaluate the effectiveness of holistic practices and address any new concerns.

- Feedback and Adaptation: Encourage feedback from the individual regarding their experiences with the holistic practices. Use this feedback to adapt and refine the treatment plan, ensuring it remains effective and aligned with the individual's needs.

Evaluating the Effectiveness of Different Holistic Approaches

EVALUATING THE EFFECTIVENESS of holistic approaches involves assessing their impact on physical, mental, and emotional well-being. This evaluation can help determine which practices are most beneficial for the individual and how they can be best integrated into the treatment plan.

1. Criteria for Evaluation

- Symptom Reduction: Assess the extent to which holistic practices reduce symptoms of compulsive behaviors and associated mental health conditions (e.g., anxiety, depression).

- Quality of Life: Evaluate improvements in overall quality of life, including physical health, emotional well-being, and daily functioning.

- Stress and Anxiety Levels: Measure changes in stress and anxiety levels through self-reports, clinical assessments, and physiological markers (e.g., heart rate, cortisol levels).

- Cognitive Function: Assess improvements in cognitive function, such as memory, attention, and executive function.

2. Methods of Evaluation

- Self-Reports: Use self-report questionnaires and journals to gather information about the individual's experiences with holistic practices. This can include their perceived benefits, challenges, and overall satisfaction.

- Clinical Assessments: Conduct regular clinical assessments to evaluate changes in symptoms and overall health. This can include standardized questionnaires, interviews, and physical examinations.

- Physiological Measures: Use physiological measures, such as heart rate variability, blood pressure, and cortisol levels, to assess the impact of holistic practices on stress and overall health.

- Behavioral Observations: Observe changes in behavior, such as increased engagement in daily activities, improved social interactions, and reduced reliance on compulsive behaviors.

3. Case Studies and Research Evidence

- Individual Case Studies: Document individual case studies to provide detailed insights into the effectiveness of holistic practices. These case studies can highlight specific strategies, outcomes, and lessons learned.

- Research Evidence: Review and incorporate research evidence on the effectiveness of holistic practices. This includes studies on acupuncture, yoga, aromatherapy, and other alternative therapies. Use evidence-based practices to inform the treatment plan.

4. Adjusting the Treatment Plan Based on Evaluation

- Identifying Effective Practices: Based on the evaluation, identify which holistic practices are most effective for the individual. Continue and enhance these practices while addressing any challenges or barriers.

- Modifying Ineffective Practices: If certain practices are not yielding the desired results, consider modifying or replacing them with alternative approaches. Adapt the treatment plan to ensure it remains effective and aligned with the individual's needs.

- Continuous Improvement: Foster a mindset of continuous improvement, regularly evaluating and refining the treatment plan. This ensures that the plan evolves to meet the individual's changing needs and goals.

Detailed Examples and Case Studies

TO ILLUSTRATE THE APPLICATION and evaluation of holistic approaches, let's explore detailed examples and case studies of individuals who have successfully integrated holistic practices into their treatment plans and experienced significant improvements in their well-being.

Case Study 1: Integrating Acupuncture for Anxiety Management

BACKGROUND: JANE IS a 35-year-old woman who has been struggling with severe anxiety and panic attacks for several years. Despite trying various medications and therapies, she continued to experience debilitating symptoms.

Holistic Approach:

1. ASSESSMENT AND PERSONALIZATION: Jane's healthcare provider conducted a comprehensive evaluation and recommended integrating acupuncture into her treatment plan to complement her existing therapy and medication.

2. Acupuncture Sessions: Jane started receiving acupuncture treatments twice a week. The sessions focused on specific points known to alleviate anxiety and promote relaxation.

3. Daily Practices: Jane incorporated daily mindfulness meditation and deep breathing exercises to enhance the effects of acupuncture.

Evaluation and Outcomes:

1. SYMPTOM REDUCTION: Over several months, Jane experienced a significant reduction in her anxiety symptoms and panic attacks. She reported feeling calmer and more in control of her emotions.

2. Quality of Life: Jane's overall quality of life improved. She was able to engage in social activities, return to work, and enjoy hobbies she had previously abandoned.

3. Stress and Anxiety Levels: Clinical assessments and self-reports indicated a marked decrease in Jane's stress and anxiety levels. Physiological measures, such as heart rate variability and cortisol levels, also showed improvement.

Feedback and Adaptation:

1. POSITIVE EXPERIENCES: Jane reported a high level of satisfaction with the acupuncture treatments. She found them to be relaxing and effective in managing her anxiety.

2. Ongoing Integration: Based on the positive outcomes, Jane's healthcare provider recommended continuing acupuncture sessions once a week as part of her long-term treatment plan.

Conclusion: Integrating acupuncture into Jane's treatment plan significantly improved her anxiety management and overall well-being. The holistic approach complemented her existing therapies and provided additional support for her mental health.

Case Study 2: Using Yoga to Manage Depression

BACKGROUND: MARK IS a 45-year-old man who has been struggling with chronic depression. He had tried various medications and therapies with limited success and was seeking additional strategies to improve his mental health.

Holistic Approach:

1. ASSESSMENT AND PERSONALIZATION: Mark's healthcare provider conducted a comprehensive evaluation and recommended incorporating yoga into his treatment plan to complement his existing medication and therapy.

2. Yoga Practice: Mark started practicing yoga three times a week, focusing on Hatha and Vinyasa styles that combined physical postures, breath control, and meditation.

3. Daily Practices: Mark included daily mindfulness meditation and journaling to enhance the effects of his yoga practice.

Evaluation and Outcomes:

1. SYMPTOM REDUCTION: Over several months, Mark experienced a significant reduction in his depression symptoms. He reported improved mood, increased energy levels, and enhanced emotional regulation.

2. Quality of Life: Mark's overall quality of life improved. He was able to engage more fully in daily activities, improve his relationships, and pursue interests and hobbies.

3. Cognitive Function: Clinical assessments indicated improvements in Mark's cognitive function, including memory, attention, and executive function.

Feedback and Adaptation:

1. POSITIVE EXPERIENCES: Mark reported a high level of satisfaction with his yoga practice. He found it to be a powerful tool for managing his depression and enhancing his overall well-being.

2. Ongoing Integration: Based on the positive outcomes, Mark's healthcare provider recommended continuing his yoga practice as part of his long-term treatment plan, with regular check-ins to monitor progress.

Conclusion: Integrating yoga into Mark's treatment plan significantly improved his depression management and overall well-being. The holistic approach complemented his existing therapies and provided additional support for his mental health.

Case Study 3: Incorporating Aromatherapy for Stress Reduction

BACKGROUND: SARAH IS a 28-year-old woman who has been struggling with chronic stress and anxiety due to her demanding job. She was looking for additional strategies to manage her stress and improve her mental health.

Holistic Approach:

1. ASSESSMENT AND PERSONALIZATION: Sarah's healthcare provider conducted a comprehensive evaluation and recommended incorporating aromatherapy into her treatment plan to complement her existing stress management techniques.

2. Aromatherapy Practices: Sarah started using essential oils, such as lavender, chamomile, and ylang-ylang, for relaxation and stress reduction. She used a diffuser in her home and office and applied diluted oils to her wrists and temples.

3. Daily Practices: Sarah incorporated daily mindfulness meditation, deep breathing exercises, and regular exercise to enhance the effects of aromatherapy.

Evaluation and Outcomes:

1. SYMPTOM REDUCTION: Over several months, Sarah experienced a significant reduction in her stress and anxiety levels. She reported feeling more relaxed and better able to manage her work-related stress.

2. Quality of Life: Sarah's overall quality of life improved. She was able to enjoy her work more, improve her productivity, and engage in social activities and hobbies.

3. Physiological Measures: Physiological measures, such as heart rate variability and cortisol levels, indicated a decrease in Sarah's stress levels.

Feedback and Adaptation:

1. POSITIVE EXPERIENCES: Sarah reported a high level of satisfaction with aromatherapy. She found it to be a convenient and effective way to manage her stress and enhance her overall well-being.

2. Ongoing Integration: Based on the positive outcomes, Sarah's healthcare provider recommended continuing the use of aromatherapy as part of her long-term stress management plan, with regular check-ins to monitor progress.

Conclusion: Integrating aromatherapy into Sarah's treatment plan significantly improved her stress management and overall well-being. The holistic approach complemented her existing stress management techniques and provided additional support for her mental health.

Conclusion

Holistic approaches to health and wellness consider the whole person—mind, body, and spirit—in the quest for optimal well-being. Alternative therapies, including acupuncture, yoga, and aromatherapy, are integral components of holistic health care. These therapies can complement traditional medical treatments and offer additional avenues for managing compulsive behaviors and enhancing mental health.

Integrating holistic practices into a comprehensive treatment plan involves combining traditional medical treatments with alternative therapies to address all aspects of an individual's well-being. This approach can enhance the effectiveness of treatment and support long-term recovery from compulsive behaviors.

Evaluating the effectiveness of holistic approaches involves assessing their impact on physical, mental, and emotional well-being. This evaluation can help determine which practices are most beneficial for the individual and how they can be best integrated into the treatment plan.

The detailed examples and case studies presented in this chapter illustrate how individuals can successfully integrate holistic practices into their treatment plans and experience significant improvements in their well-being. By incorporating these strategies into their lives, individuals can achieve meaningful and lasting improvements in their mental health. With the right tools, techniques, and support, it is possible to overcome the challenges posed by mental health conditions and work towards a healthier, more balanced future.

Chapter 13: Success Stories

Inspiring Stories of Individuals Who Have Overcome Compulsive Behaviors

In the journey towards overcoming compulsive behaviors, hearing about the successes of others can provide powerful motivation and hope. The following stories highlight the resilience, determination, and transformative strategies that have enabled individuals to reclaim their lives from the grip of compulsive behaviors.

Story 1: Sarah's Triumph Over Compulsive Eating

BACKGROUND: SARAH HAD struggled with compulsive eating since her teenage years. Whenever she felt stressed or emotional, she turned to food for comfort, leading to significant weight gain and health issues. Despite numerous attempts to control her eating habits, Sarah found herself trapped in a cycle of binge eating and guilt.

Turning Point:

1. Seeking Professional Help: Sarah decided to seek help from a therapist specializing in eating disorders. This was a crucial step in understanding the underlying emotional triggers of her behavior.

2. Joining a Support Group: Sarah joined a support group for individuals with compulsive eating issues. Sharing her experiences with others who understood her struggles provided much-needed support and encouragement.

Strategies That Worked:

1. Cognitive-Behavioral Therapy (CBT): Sarah's therapist introduced her to CBT, which helped her identify and challenge the irrational thoughts driving

her compulsive eating. By reframing these thoughts, she learned healthier ways to cope with stress and emotions.

2. Mindfulness and Meditation: Incorporating mindfulness and meditation into her daily routine helped Sarah become more aware of her eating triggers and develop better self-control. Mindful eating allowed her to savor each bite and recognize when she was truly hungry.

3. Balanced Nutrition: With the guidance of a nutritionist, Sarah developed a balanced meal plan that provided the nutrients her body needed without triggering overeating. She focused on whole foods, including plenty of fruits, vegetables, lean proteins, and whole grains.

Outcome:

Over time, Sarah's relationship with food transformed. She lost weight, improved her physical health, and gained a new sense of control over her eating habits. The support group remained a crucial part of her journey, offering ongoing encouragement and accountability.

Lessons Learned:

- Seeking professional help can provide valuable insights and strategies.

- Support groups offer a sense of community and shared understanding.

- Mindfulness practices can enhance self-awareness and control.

Story 2: Mark's Victory Over Compulsive Shopping

BACKGROUND: MARK'S compulsive shopping habits had spiraled out of control, leading to financial problems and strained relationships. Whenever he felt anxious or bored, he turned to shopping as a way to fill the void. His home was cluttered with unnecessary purchases, and he faced mounting debt.

Turning Point:

1. Financial Crisis: A financial crisis forced Mark to confront the consequences of his compulsive shopping. Realizing the extent of his problem, he decided to seek help.

2. Professional Guidance: Mark enlisted the help of a financial advisor and a therapist specializing in compulsive behaviors. This combination of financial and psychological support was essential for his recovery.

Strategies That Worked:

1. Budgeting and Financial Planning: With the help of his financial advisor, Mark developed a strict budget and financial plan. He learned to track his expenses, prioritize essential spending, and avoid impulse purchases.

2. Cognitive-Behavioral Therapy (CBT): Mark's therapist used CBT to help him identify the emotional triggers behind his shopping habits. By addressing these underlying issues, he developed healthier ways to cope with stress and boredom.

3. Mindfulness Practices: Mark incorporated mindfulness practices, such as meditation and deep breathing exercises, into his daily routine. These practices helped him manage anxiety and reduce the urge to shop compulsively.

Outcome:

Mark successfully reduced his compulsive shopping habits, paid off his debt, and decluttered his home. He regained control over his finances and rebuilt trust in his relationships. The combination of financial planning and psychological support was key to his recovery.

Lessons Learned:

- Financial planning is crucial for managing compulsive shopping.

- Addressing underlying emotional triggers can lead to lasting change.

- Mindfulness practices can help manage anxiety and reduce compulsive urges.

Story 3: Emily's Success in Overcoming Compulsive

Hoarding

BACKGROUND: EMILY'S home was filled with items she couldn't bring herself to discard, including old newspapers, clothing, and broken appliances. Her compulsive hoarding had reached a point where most rooms were unusable, and her living conditions were hazardous.

Turning Point:

1. Family Intervention: Emily's family staged an intervention, expressing their concern for her health and safety. This wake-up call prompted Emily to seek help.

2. Professional Support: Emily sought help from a therapist specializing in hoarding disorder. She also enlisted the assistance of a professional organizer to help her declutter her home.

Strategies That Worked:

1. Cognitive-Behavioral Therapy (CBT): Emily's therapist used CBT to address the emotional attachments and irrational beliefs driving her hoarding behavior. She learned to challenge these thoughts and develop healthier coping mechanisms.

2. Decluttering Plan: With the help of a professional organizer, Emily developed a structured decluttering plan. They tackled one room at a time, sorting items into categories (keep, donate, discard) and gradually creating a more functional living space.

3. Support Groups: Emily joined a support group for individuals with hoarding disorder. Sharing her experiences and hearing from others facing similar challenges provided motivation and support.

Outcome:

Emily made significant progress in decluttering her home and managing her hoarding behavior. Her living conditions improved, and she regained a sense of control over her environment. The support of her family, therapist, and support group was instrumental in her recovery.

Lessons Learned:

- Family support and professional intervention can be powerful motivators for change.

- A structured decluttering plan can make the process more manageable.

- Support groups offer valuable encouragement and shared experiences.

Story 4: John's Journey to Overcoming Substance Abuse

BACKGROUND: JOHN STRUGGLED with substance abuse for many years, using alcohol and drugs to cope with stress and emotional pain. His addiction affected his relationships, career, and health, leading to a downward spiral.

Turning Point:

1. Health Scare: A serious health scare prompted John to seek help. Realizing the impact of his substance abuse on his well-being, he decided to take action.

2. Rehabilitation Program: John enrolled in a rehabilitation program that provided comprehensive support, including medical treatment, therapy, and peer support.

Strategies That Worked:

1. Detox and Medical Treatment: The rehabilitation program included a medically supervised detox process to help John safely withdraw from substances. Ongoing medical support addressed his physical health needs.

2. Cognitive-Behavioral Therapy (CBT): John participated in CBT sessions to address the underlying emotional issues driving his substance abuse. He learned healthier ways to cope with stress and emotions.

3. Support Groups: John attended support group meetings, such as Alcoholics Anonymous (AA) and Narcotics Anonymous (NA). These groups provided a sense of community, accountability, and encouragement.

Outcome:

John successfully completed the rehabilitation program and maintained his sobriety. He rebuilt his relationships, pursued a fulfilling career, and improved his overall health. The combination of medical treatment, therapy, and peer support was crucial to his recovery.

Lessons Learned:

- Comprehensive rehabilitation programs can provide essential medical and psychological support.

- Addressing underlying emotional issues is key to overcoming substance abuse.

- Support groups offer valuable community and accountability.

Story 5: Rachel's Triumph Over Compulsive Skin Picking

BACKGROUND: RACHEL had struggled with compulsive skin picking (dermatillomania) since her teenage years. She often picked at her skin to cope with stress and anxiety, leading to physical damage and emotional distress.

Turning Point:

1. Dermatological Advice: A visit to a dermatologist highlighted the physical consequences of her behavior and prompted Rachel to seek help for her skin picking.

2. Therapeutic Support: Rachel sought help from a therapist specializing in body-focused repetitive behaviors (BFRBs). This was a crucial step in understanding and addressing her compulsive skin picking.

Strategies That Worked:

1. Cognitive-Behavioral Therapy (CBT): Rachel's therapist used CBT to help her identify the triggers and irrational thoughts driving her skin picking. By addressing these underlying issues, Rachel developed healthier coping mechanisms.

2. Habit Reversal Training (HRT): Rachel learned habit reversal training techniques, such as substituting skin picking with healthier behaviors (e.g., squeezing a stress ball). This helped reduce the frequency and intensity of her skin picking.

3. Mindfulness Practices: Rachel incorporated mindfulness practices, such as meditation and deep breathing exercises, into her daily routine. These practices helped her manage stress and become more aware of her picking triggers.

Outcome:

Over time, Rachel successfully reduced her compulsive skin picking and improved the condition of her skin. She gained a new sense of control over her behavior and enhanced her emotional well-being. The combination of CBT, HRT, and mindfulness practices was key to her recovery.

Lessons Learned:

- Professional support can provide valuable insights and strategies for managing BFRBs.

- Habit reversal training can help replace compulsive behaviors with healthier alternatives.

- Mindfulness practices can enhance self-awareness and stress management.

Lessons Learned and Strategies That Worked

THE SUCCESS STORIES highlighted in this chapter illustrate the resilience, determination, and transformative strategies that have enabled individuals to reclaim their lives from the grip of compulsive behaviors. Here are some common lessons learned and strategies that worked for them:

1. Seeking Professional Help: Many individuals found that seeking help from therapists, counselors, and other healthcare professionals was a crucial step in their recovery. Professional support provided valuable insights, strategies, and guidance for managing compulsive behaviors.

2. Support Groups: Joining support groups offered a sense of community, shared understanding, and encouragement. Support groups provided a platform for individuals to share their experiences, learn from others, and gain motivation.

3. Cognitive-Behavioral Therapy (CBT): CBT was a common and effective therapy for addressing the underlying thoughts and emotions driving compulsive behaviors. By challenging and reframing irrational thoughts, individuals developed healthier coping mechanisms.

4. Mindfulness Practices: Incorporating mindfulness practices, such as meditation and deep breathing exercises, helped individuals become more aware of their triggers and manage stress. Mindfulness practices enhanced self-awareness and emotional regulation.

5. Structured Plans: Developing structured plans for managing compulsive behaviors, such as budgeting for compulsive shopping or creating a decluttering plan for hoarding, made the process more manageable and achievable.

6. Combining Approaches: Many individuals benefited from combining traditional therapies with holistic practices, such as yoga, acupuncture, and aromatherapy. These complementary approaches provided additional support for physical and emotional well-being.

7. Perseverance and Hope: Maintaining hope and perseverance was essential for overcoming setbacks and staying committed to recovery. Individuals found that believing in their ability to change and persevering through challenges was key to their success.

The Importance of Hope and Perseverance

HOPE AND PERSEVERANCE are critical components of the recovery journey. Overcoming compulsive behaviors often involves setbacks and challenges, but maintaining a hopeful and determined mindset can make a significant difference. Here are some reasons why hope and perseverance are essential:

1. Motivation: Hope provides the motivation to keep moving forward, even when progress seems slow or setbacks occur. Believing that recovery is possible inspires individuals to stay committed to their goals.

2. Resilience: Perseverance builds resilience, enabling individuals to bounce back from setbacks and continue working towards recovery. It helps them navigate challenges and maintain a positive outlook.

3. Empowerment: Hope empowers individuals to take control of their lives and make positive changes. It fosters a sense of agency and confidence in their ability to overcome compulsive behaviors.

4. Support: Maintaining hope and perseverance can inspire others and strengthen support networks. When individuals demonstrate resilience and determination, it encourages their loved ones and support groups to continue offering support and encouragement.

5. Long-Term Success: Recovery from compulsive behaviors is often a long-term process. Hope and perseverance are essential for sustaining the effort needed to achieve lasting change and maintain progress.

Conclusion

The success stories highlighted in this chapter demonstrate the resilience, determination, and transformative strategies that have enabled individuals to overcome compulsive behaviors and reclaim their lives. By seeking professional help, joining support groups, practicing cognitive-behavioral therapy, incorporating mindfulness practices, and developing structured plans, these individuals achieved meaningful and lasting recovery.

Maintaining hope and perseverance was crucial to their success. Believing in their ability to change and staying committed to their recovery goals allowed them to navigate setbacks and challenges. The importance of hope and perseverance cannot be overstated in the journey towards overcoming compulsive behaviors.

By learning from these success stories and incorporating the strategies and lessons learned, individuals can find inspiration and motivation to continue their own recovery journey. With the right support, resilience, and determination, it is possible to overcome the challenges posed by compulsive behaviors and work towards a healthier, more balanced future.

Chapter 14: Creating a Long-Term Plan

Developing a Sustainable Lifestyle to Prevent Recurrence

Long-term recovery from compulsive behaviors requires more than short-term fixes; it necessitates the development of a sustainable lifestyle that supports mental, emotional, and physical well-being. By fostering habits that promote health and resilience, individuals can reduce the risk of recurrence and maintain their progress.

1. Understanding the Foundations of a Sustainable Lifestyle

- Balance and Moderation: A sustainable lifestyle is one of balance and moderation. This includes balancing work and leisure, physical activity and rest, and healthy eating with occasional treats. Striving for moderation helps prevent burnout and reduces the risk of relapse.

- Routine and Structure: Establishing a daily routine provides structure and stability, which can be particularly beneficial for those recovering from compulsive behaviors. Regular schedules for meals, exercise, work, and relaxation create a predictable environment that supports healthy habits.

- Holistic Health: Focusing on holistic health involves addressing physical, mental, and emotional needs. This includes proper nutrition, regular physical activity, mental health care, and emotional well-being practices.

2. Key Components of a Sustainable Lifestyle

- Nutrition: A balanced diet rich in essential nutrients supports overall health and well-being. Emphasize whole foods, including fruits, vegetables, lean proteins, whole grains, and healthy fats. Avoid excessive consumption of processed foods, sugars, and unhealthy fats.

- Physical Activity: Regular exercise is crucial for maintaining physical health and mental well-being. Aim for a mix of aerobic activities, strength training, and flexibility exercises. Find activities you enjoy to make exercise a regular part of your routine.

- Sleep: Adequate sleep is essential for physical and mental health. Establish a regular sleep schedule, create a restful sleep environment, and practice good sleep hygiene. Aim for 7-9 hours of sleep per night.

- Stress Management: Effective stress management techniques, such as mindfulness, meditation, deep breathing exercises, and hobbies, help reduce the risk of relapse. Identify stressors and develop strategies to manage them proactively.

- Social Support: Maintain strong social connections with family, friends, and support groups. Regular social interactions provide emotional support, accountability, and a sense of belonging.

- Mental Health Care: Regular mental health care, including therapy, counseling, or support groups, helps address underlying issues and supports ongoing recovery. Consider periodic check-ins with a mental health professional to maintain progress.

3. Implementing and Maintaining a Sustainable Lifestyle

- Start Small: Begin with small, manageable changes to avoid feeling overwhelmed. Gradually incorporate new habits into your routine, building on your successes over time.

- Consistency is Key: Consistency is crucial for maintaining a sustainable lifestyle. Stick to your routine even when life gets busy or stressful. Consistent practice helps solidify new habits and makes them second nature.

- Flexibility and Adaptability: While consistency is important, it's also essential to remain flexible and adaptable. Life circumstances can change, and being able to adjust your routine accordingly helps maintain your overall well-being.

- Regular Reflection and Adjustment: Periodically reflect on your lifestyle and make adjustments as needed. Assess what is working well and what could be improved. This ongoing evaluation helps ensure that your lifestyle remains supportive of your long-term recovery.

Setting Long-Term Goals and Milestones

SETTING LONG-TERM GOALS and milestones provides direction, motivation, and a sense of accomplishment in the recovery journey. Clear, achievable goals help maintain focus and drive progress, while milestones celebrate achievements and reinforce commitment to recovery.

1. The Importance of Long-Term Goals

- Direction and Purpose: Long-term goals provide a sense of direction and purpose, guiding your efforts and decisions. They help you stay focused on what you want to achieve and why it matters.

- Motivation and Drive: Having clear goals motivates you to keep moving forward, even when faced with challenges. They provide a reason to persevere and work towards positive change.

- Measuring Progress: Goals allow you to measure progress and assess your achievements. Tracking your progress provides a sense of accomplishment and encourages continued effort.

2. Setting Effective Long-Term Goals

- SMART Goals: Ensure your goals are Specific, Measurable, Achievable, Relevant, and Time-bound (SMART). This framework helps create clear and attainable objectives.

- Specific: Clearly define what you want to achieve. For example, instead of setting a vague goal like "get healthier," specify "exercise for 30 minutes, five days a week."

- Measurable: Establish criteria to track your progress. This could be the number of workouts completed each week or the amount of weight lifted.

- Achievable: Set goals that are challenging yet attainable. Consider your current capabilities and resources when setting goals.

- Relevant: Ensure that your goals align with your values and long-term objectives. Ask yourself why the goal is important and how it contributes to your overall well-being.

- Time-bound: Set a deadline or timeframe for achieving your goals. This adds a sense of urgency and helps maintain focus.

3. Breaking Down Long-Term Goals into Milestones

- Short-Term Goals: Divide your long-term goals into short-term objectives. Short-term goals provide immediate targets to work towards, making the overall goal more manageable.

- Actionable Steps: Break down each goal into smaller, actionable steps. This makes the goal more manageable and reduces the likelihood of feeling overwhelmed.

- Celebrating Milestones: Celebrate milestones and achievements along the way. Acknowledging progress, no matter how small, reinforces positive behavior and boosts motivation.

4. Examples of Long-Term Goals and Milestones

- Physical Health Goal: Improve physical fitness and strength.

- Milestones: Complete a fitness assessment, set a baseline, establish a workout routine, increase workout intensity, achieve specific fitness benchmarks (e.g., run a 5K, lift a certain weight).

- Mental Health Goal: Reduce symptoms of anxiety and depression.

- Milestones: Start therapy, practice mindfulness daily, track mood changes, learn and apply coping strategies, reduce frequency and intensity of symptoms.

- Career Goal: Advance in your career or pursue a new professional path.

- Milestones: Identify career goals, update resume, seek additional training or education, apply for new positions, achieve career milestones (e.g., promotion, new job).

- Personal Development Goal: Develop a new skill or hobby.

- Milestones: Choose a skill or hobby, gather necessary materials, set a practice schedule, track progress, achieve specific skill levels or milestones (e.g., complete a project, participate in a competition).

Continual Self-Improvement and Personal Growth

CONTINUAL SELF-IMPROVEMENT and personal growth are essential components of maintaining long-term recovery and overall well-being. By striving for ongoing development, individuals can build resilience, enhance their skills, and achieve a greater sense of fulfillment.

1. The Importance of Continual Self-Improvement

- Adaptability and Resilience: Continual self-improvement helps build adaptability and resilience, enabling individuals to navigate challenges and setbacks more effectively.

- Personal Fulfillment: Pursuing personal growth leads to a greater sense of fulfillment and satisfaction. It encourages individuals to reach their full potential and live meaningful lives.

- Enhanced Skills and Abilities: Ongoing development enhances skills and abilities, contributing to personal and professional success. It opens up new opportunities and broadens horizons.

2. Strategies for Continual Self-Improvement

- Lifelong Learning: Commit to lifelong learning by seeking new knowledge and skills. This can include formal education, online courses, workshops, reading, and self-study. Stay curious and open to new experiences.

- Setting Growth-Oriented Goals: Set goals that focus on personal growth and development. These can include learning a new language, developing a new hobby, or improving a specific skill.

- Seeking Feedback: Regularly seek feedback from others to gain insights into your strengths and areas for improvement. Constructive feedback helps identify opportunities for growth and development.

- Reflecting and Journaling: Reflect on your experiences and progress through journaling. Regular reflection helps identify patterns, recognize achievements, and set new goals.

- Practicing Self-Compassion: Embrace self-compassion and acknowledge that growth involves setbacks and challenges. Be kind to yourself and view mistakes as opportunities for learning.

3. Examples of Continual Self-Improvement Activities

- Educational Pursuits: Enroll in courses or workshops to gain new knowledge and skills. This could include learning a new language, pursuing higher education, or taking up a new hobby.

- Creative Endeavors: Engage in creative activities such as writing, painting, music, or crafting. Creative pursuits provide a sense of accomplishment and enhance problem-solving skills.

- Physical Challenges: Set physical challenges that push your limits and improve your fitness. This could include training for a marathon, taking up a new sport, or achieving specific fitness milestones.

- Volunteer Work: Participate in volunteer work or community service. Volunteering provides a sense of purpose, enhances social connections, and contributes to personal growth.

- Mindfulness and Meditation: Practice mindfulness and meditation to enhance self-awareness and emotional regulation. These practices promote mental clarity and resilience.

4. Creating a Supportive Environment for Personal Growth

- Surround Yourself with Positive Influences: Build a support network of individuals who encourage and inspire you. Positive influences provide motivation and support for personal growth.

- Engage in Continuous Learning: Stay engaged in continuous learning by seeking out new experiences and challenges. This could include attending workshops, joining clubs or groups, and exploring new interests.

- Embrace Change: Be open to change and willing to step out of your comfort zone. Embracing change fosters personal growth and opens up new opportunities.

- Celebrate Your Achievements: Celebrate your achievements and milestones, no matter how small. Recognizing your progress boosts motivation and reinforces positive behavior.

Detailed Examples and Case Studies

TO ILLUSTRATE THE DEVELOPMENT of a sustainable lifestyle, setting long-term goals and milestones, and continual self-improvement, let's explore detailed examples and case studies of individuals who have successfully implemented these strategies and maintained their recovery.

Case Study 1: Developing a Sustainable Lifestyle

BACKGROUND: EMILY HAD struggled with compulsive eating for many years. After seeking therapy and joining a support group, she made significant progress in managing her eating habits. Emily wanted to develop a sustainable lifestyle to maintain her progress and prevent recurrence.

Developing a Sustainable Lifestyle:

1. BALANCED NUTRITION: Emily worked with a nutritionist to develop a balanced meal plan that provided the nutrients her body needed. She focused

on whole foods, including plenty of fruits, vegetables, lean proteins, and whole grains.

2. Regular Exercise: Emily incorporated regular exercise into her routine, including a mix of aerobic activities, strength training, and yoga. She found activities she enjoyed, such as dancing and hiking, to make exercise enjoyable.

3. Sleep Hygiene: Emily established a regular sleep schedule and created a restful sleep environment. She aimed for 7-9 hours of sleep per night to support her physical and mental health.

4. Stress Management: Emily practiced mindfulness and meditation daily to manage stress. She also engaged in hobbies, such as painting and gardening, to relax and unwind.

5. Social Support: Emily maintained strong social connections with family, friends, and her support group. Regular social interactions provided emotional support and accountability.

Outcome:

Over time, Emily successfully developed a sustainable lifestyle that supported her long-term recovery. She maintained her progress, improved her physical and mental health, and reduced the risk of recurrence.

Case Study 2: Setting Long-Term Goals and Milestones

BACKGROUND: MARK HAD struggled with compulsive shopping for many years, leading to financial problems and strained relationships. After seeking help from a financial advisor and therapist, he wanted to set long-term goals and milestones to maintain his progress.

Setting Long-Term Goals and Milestones:

1. FINANCIAL HEALTH Goal: Improve financial stability and reduce debt.

- Milestones: Complete a financial assessment, set a budget, track expenses, reduce debt by 20%, achieve financial milestones (e.g., build an emergency fund, save for a major purchase).

2. Personal Development Goal: Develop a new skill or hobby.

- Milestones: Choose a skill or hobby, gather necessary materials, set a practice schedule, track progress, achieve specific skill levels or milestones (e.g., complete a project, participate in a competition).

Outcome:

Mark successfully set and achieved his long-term goals and milestones. He improved his financial stability, reduced debt, and developed new skills and hobbies. Setting clear goals and milestones provided direction, motivation, and a sense of accomplishment.

Case Study 3: Continual Self-Improvement and Personal Growth

BACKGROUND: SARAH HAD struggled with substance abuse for many years. After completing a rehabilitation program, she wanted to focus on continual self-improvement and personal growth to maintain her sobriety and enhance her overall well-being.

Continual Self-Improvement and Personal Growth:

1. LIFELONG LEARNING: Sarah enrolled in online courses to gain new knowledge and skills. She pursued higher education and took up new hobbies, such as photography and cooking.

2. Creative Endeavors: Sarah engaged in creative activities, such as writing and painting, to express herself and enhance her problem-solving skills.

3. Physical Challenges: Sarah set physical challenges, such as training for a marathon and taking up rock climbing, to improve her fitness and push her limits.

4. Volunteer Work: Sarah participated in volunteer work, helping at a local shelter and mentoring others in recovery. Volunteering provided a sense of purpose and enhanced her social connections.

5. Mindfulness and Meditation: Sarah practiced mindfulness and meditation daily to enhance self-awareness and emotional regulation. These practices promoted mental clarity and resilience.

Outcome:

Sarah successfully focused on continual self-improvement and personal growth. She maintained her sobriety, improved her physical and mental health, and achieved a greater sense of fulfillment. The pursuit of lifelong learning, creative endeavors, physical challenges, volunteer work, and mindfulness practices contributed to her ongoing development and well-being.

Conclusion

Creating a long-term plan for maintaining recovery from compulsive behaviors involves developing a sustainable lifestyle, setting long-term goals and milestones, and focusing on continual self-improvement and personal growth. By fostering habits that promote health and resilience, individuals can reduce the risk of recurrence and maintain their progress.

A sustainable lifestyle includes balanced nutrition, regular exercise, adequate sleep, stress management, social support, and mental health care. Setting long-term goals and milestones provides direction, motivation, and a sense of accomplishment. Continual self-improvement and personal growth enhance adaptability, resilience, and personal fulfillment.

The detailed examples and case studies presented in this chapter illustrate how individuals can successfully develop a sustainable lifestyle, set and achieve long-term goals, and focus on continual self-improvement. By incorporating these strategies into their lives, individuals can achieve meaningful and lasting recovery from compulsive behaviors. With the right tools, techniques, and support, it is possible to overcome the challenges posed by compulsive behaviors and work towards a healthier, more balanced future.

Chapter 15: Conclusion and Moving Forward

Recap of Key Concepts and Strategies

As we conclude this journey through understanding and overcoming compulsive behaviors, it's essential to recap the key concepts and strategies discussed throughout the book. These principles and tools form the foundation for managing and recovering from compulsive behaviors, providing a roadmap for sustained well-being and personal growth.

1. Understanding Compulsive Behaviors

- Definition and Types: Compulsive behaviors are repetitive actions driven by an overwhelming urge, often used as a coping mechanism for stress, anxiety, or other emotional challenges. Types of compulsive behaviors include substance abuse, eating disorders, compulsive shopping, hoarding, and more.

- Neurological and Psychological Foundations: Compulsive behaviors are influenced by both neurological and psychological factors. The brain's reward system plays a crucial role, with neurotransmitters like dopamine reinforcing the compulsive actions. Psychological factors, such as past trauma and emotional distress, also contribute to the development and maintenance of these behaviors.

2. Identifying Compulsive Behaviors

- Signs and Symptoms: Recognizing the signs and symptoms of compulsive behaviors is the first step toward recovery. These may include a preoccupation with the behavior, loss of control, and continuing the behavior despite negative consequences.

- Self-Assessment Tools: Utilizing self-assessment tools and techniques helps individuals identify the presence and extent of their compulsive behaviors. These tools can provide insight into patterns and triggers, facilitating a deeper understanding of the underlying issues.

3. The Emotional Toll of Compulsive Behaviors

- Emotional and Mental Health Consequences: Compulsive behaviors often lead to significant emotional and mental health challenges, including anxiety, depression, guilt, and shame. These behaviors can strain relationships and impact daily functioning.

- Cycle of Shame and Guilt: Understanding the cycle of shame and guilt associated with compulsive behaviors is crucial. Breaking this cycle involves developing self-compassion and seeking professional help to address underlying emotional issues.

4. Seeking Professional Help

- Types of Therapy and Counseling: Various therapeutic approaches, including cognitive-behavioral therapy (CBT), dialectical behavior therapy (DBT), and motivational interviewing, have proven effective in treating compulsive behaviors. Choosing the right type of therapy depends on individual needs and preferences.

- Medication Options: Medications, such as antidepressants and anti-anxiety drugs, can be beneficial in managing symptoms associated with compulsive behaviors. It's important to consult a healthcare professional to determine the appropriate medication and dosage.

- Finding the Right Therapist or Support Group: Seeking professional help and finding a suitable therapist or support group is vital for recovery. These professionals and groups provide guidance, support, and accountability throughout the healing process.

5. Cognitive-Behavioral Strategies

- Cognitive-Behavioral Therapy (CBT): CBT is a widely used therapeutic approach that focuses on identifying and challenging irrational thoughts and beliefs. It helps individuals develop healthier thought patterns and behaviors.

- Practical Exercises for Behavior Modification: Implementing practical exercises, such as exposure therapy, behavioral activation, and mindfulness practices, can aid in modifying compulsive behaviors. These techniques promote self-awareness and emotional regulation.

6. Mindfulness and Meditation

- Role of Mindfulness: Mindfulness involves being present in the moment and observing thoughts and feelings without judgment. It helps individuals manage compulsive urges and develop healthier coping mechanisms.

- Meditation Techniques: Incorporating meditation techniques, such as mindful breathing, body scan, and loving-kindness meditation, enhances self-awareness and control. These practices promote relaxation and reduce stress.

7. Building Healthy Habits

- Replacing Compulsive Behaviors: Developing healthy habits involves replacing compulsive behaviors with positive alternatives. This process requires identifying triggers, setting realistic goals, and maintaining consistency.

- Goal Setting and Progress Tracking: Setting long-term goals and tracking progress provides motivation and a sense of accomplishment. Celebrating milestones reinforces positive behavior and encourages continued effort.

8. The Power of Support Networks

- Building a Support System: A strong support network, including family, friends, and support groups, is crucial for recovery. These networks provide emotional support, accountability, and encouragement.

- Role of Family and Friends: Family and friends play a significant role in recovery by offering practical assistance, emotional support, and setting healthy boundaries.

- Joining Support Groups: Support groups offer a sense of community and shared understanding. They provide a platform for sharing experiences, learning from others, and gaining motivation.

9. Dealing with Relapse

- Understanding Relapse: Relapse is a common part of the recovery process and should be viewed as a learning opportunity rather than a failure. Understanding triggers and developing a relapse prevention plan is essential.

- Strategies for Managing Relapse: Effective strategies for managing relapse include identifying triggers, building resilience, seeking support, and reflecting on setbacks to learn and adapt.

- Learning from Setbacks: Reflecting on setbacks and adjusting strategies helps individuals move forward and strengthen their recovery. Maintaining hope and perseverance is crucial for long-term success.

10. Nutrition and Exercise

- Impact on Mental Health: Proper nutrition and regular exercise play a critical role in maintaining mental health and mitigating the symptoms of compulsive behaviors. They support brain function, reduce stress, and enhance overall well-being.

- Nutritional Tips: A balanced diet rich in essential nutrients, such as omega-3 fatty acids, B vitamins, and antioxidants, supports brain health and emotional regulation.

- Exercise Routines: Regular physical activity, including aerobic exercise, strength training, and mindfulness practices, reduces stress, improves mood, and enhances cognitive function.

11. Holistic Approaches

- Alternative Therapies: Holistic approaches, such as acupuncture, yoga, and aromatherapy, complement traditional medical treatments and provide additional support for mental health and well-being.

- Integrating Holistic Practices: Combining traditional and holistic treatments creates a comprehensive plan that addresses all aspects of an individual's well-being.

- Evaluating Effectiveness: Regularly assessing the impact of holistic practices helps determine their effectiveness and guides adjustments to the treatment plan.

12. Success Stories

- Inspiring Stories: Hearing about the successes of others provides motivation and hope. Success stories highlight the resilience and determination required to overcome compulsive behaviors.

- Lessons Learned: Key lessons from success stories include the importance of seeking professional help, joining support groups, practicing cognitive-behavioral strategies, and maintaining hope and perseverance.

- Importance of Hope and Perseverance: Maintaining hope and perseverance is essential for navigating setbacks and staying committed to recovery. Believing in the possibility of change inspires ongoing effort and resilience.

13. Creating a Long-Term Plan

- Sustainable Lifestyle: Developing a sustainable lifestyle involves balanced nutrition, regular exercise, adequate sleep, stress management, social support, and mental health care.

- Long-Term Goals and Milestones: Setting long-term goals and milestones provides direction, motivation, and a sense of accomplishment. Breaking down goals into manageable steps and celebrating progress reinforces positive behavior.

- Continual Self-Improvement: Focusing on continual self-improvement and personal growth enhances adaptability, resilience, and personal fulfillment. Pursuing lifelong learning, creative endeavors, physical challenges, and mindfulness practices contributes to ongoing development.

Encouragement and Motivation for Readers

AS YOU EMBARK ON OR continue your journey towards overcoming compulsive behaviors, it's important to remember that recovery is a process that requires time, effort, and resilience. Each step you take, no matter how small, brings you closer to a healthier and more balanced life. Here are some key points of encouragement and motivation to keep you inspired:

1. Believe in Yourself: Believe in your ability to change and grow. You have the strength and resilience to overcome challenges and create a fulfilling life. Trust in your capacity for recovery and embrace the journey ahead.

2. Embrace the Process: Recovery is a journey, not a destination. Embrace each step of the process, recognizing that progress may be gradual and nonlinear. Celebrate small victories and learn from setbacks. Every experience contributes to your growth and resilience.

3. Seek Support: You don't have to navigate this journey alone. Reach out to family, friends, support groups, and professionals who can provide guidance, encouragement, and accountability. Building a strong support network is essential for maintaining motivation and sustaining progress.

4. Stay Committed: Stay committed to your goals and the strategies that support your recovery. Consistency and perseverance are key to achieving lasting change. Even when faced with obstacles, remind yourself of the progress you've made and the potential for continued growth.

5. Practice Self-Compassion: Be kind to yourself throughout the recovery process. Practice self-compassion and recognize that setbacks are a natural part of the journey. Treat yourself with the same understanding and patience you would offer to a friend.

6. Focus on Personal Growth: Recovery is not just about overcoming compulsive behaviors; it's also about personal growth and self-improvement. Pursue new interests, develop new skills, and embrace opportunities for learning and development. A focus on growth enhances your overall well-being and sense of fulfillment.

7. Maintain Hope: Hope is a powerful motivator that sustains you through challenges and inspires you to keep moving forward. Maintain hope and

optimism, believing in the possibility of a brighter future. Your journey towards recovery is filled with potential and promise.

Resources for Further Reading and Support

TO SUPPORT YOUR ONGOING recovery journey, here are some valuable resources for further reading and support. These books, websites, and organizations offer additional insights, strategies, and community connections to help you navigate and sustain your recovery.

Books:

1. "The Mindfulness Workbook for Addiction: A Guide to Coping with the Grief, Stress, and Anger that Trigger Addictive Behaviors" by Rebecca E. Williams and Julie S. Kraft: This workbook offers practical exercises and mindfulness techniques to address the emotional triggers of addictive behaviors.

2. "The Dialectical Behavior Therapy Skills Workbook: Practical DBT Exercises for Learning Mindfulness, Interpersonal Effectiveness, Emotion Regulation & Distress Tolerance" by Matthew McKay, Jeffrey C. Wood, and Jeffrey Brantley: This workbook provides DBT exercises to help manage emotions, improve relationships, and develop coping skills.

3. "Atomic Habits: An Easy & Proven Way to Build Good Habits & Break Bad Ones" by James Clear: This book offers practical strategies for developing good habits and breaking bad ones, emphasizing the power of small changes for lasting impact.

4. "The Gifts of Imperfection: Let Go of Who You Think You're Supposed to Be and Embrace Who You Are" by Brené Brown: This book explores the importance of self-compassion, vulnerability, and embracing imperfection in the journey towards personal growth and fulfillment.

5. "Self-Compassion: The Proven Power of Being Kind to Yourself" by Kristin Neff: This book provides insights and exercises for developing self-compassion, which is essential for overcoming compulsive behaviors and fostering resilience.

Websites and Online Resources:

1. NATIONAL INSTITUTE on Drug Abuse (NIDA): www.drugabuse.gov: Provides information and resources on substance abuse, addiction, and treatment.

2. National Eating Disorders Association (NEDA): www.nationaleatingdisorders.org: Offers support, resources, and information for individuals struggling with eating disorders.

3. Alcoholics Anonymous (AA): www.aa.org: Provides information about AA meetings, resources for recovery, and support for individuals dealing with alcohol addiction.

4. Mindful: www.mindful.org: Offers resources, articles, and guided meditations for incorporating mindfulness into daily life.

5. The Anxiety and Depression Association of America (ADAA): www.adaa.org: Provides information, resources, and support for individuals dealing with anxiety, depression, and related disorders.

Support Organizations:

1. SMART RECOVERY: www.smartrecovery.org: Offers a science-based approach to addiction recovery with meetings, resources, and tools for managing addictive behaviors.

2. Celebrate Recovery: www.celebraterecovery.com: A Christian-based recovery program that provides support groups and resources for overcoming addiction and compulsive behaviors.

3. National Alliance on Mental Illness (NAMI): www.nami.org: Provides education, support, and advocacy for individuals and families affected by mental illness.

4. Hoarding Cleanup: www.hoardingcleanup.com: Offers resources and support for individuals dealing with hoarding disorder, including professional cleanup services and support groups.

5. International OCD Foundation (IOCDF): www.iocdf.org: Provides information, resources, and support for individuals with obsessive-compulsive disorder (OCD) and related disorders.

Moving Forward

AS YOU MOVE FORWARD on your journey of recovery, remember that each step you take, no matter how small, brings you closer to a healthier and more balanced life. Recovery is a continuous process that requires dedication, resilience, and self-compassion. Embrace the journey with an open heart and mind, and know that you have the strength and resources to achieve lasting change.

1. Embrace Lifelong Learning: Continue to seek knowledge and personal growth. Embrace opportunities for learning, development, and self-improvement. Lifelong learning enhances your resilience and adaptability, supporting your long-term recovery.

2. Cultivate Resilience: Build resilience by developing healthy coping mechanisms, maintaining a strong support network, and practicing self-care. Resilience helps you navigate challenges and setbacks with greater ease and confidence.

3. Stay Connected: Maintain strong connections with family, friends, and support groups. These connections provide emotional support, accountability, and a sense of belonging. Regular social interactions contribute to your overall well-being and recovery.

4. Celebrate Your Progress: Acknowledge and celebrate your achievements, no matter how small. Recognizing your progress boosts motivation and reinforces

positive behavior. Celebrate each milestone and use it as a stepping stone towards further growth.

5. Practice Self-Compassion: Treat yourself with kindness and understanding. Practice self-compassion and recognize that recovery involves setbacks and challenges. Be patient with yourself and view mistakes as opportunities for learning and growth.

6. Maintain Hope and Perseverance: Keep hope and perseverance at the forefront of your journey. Believe in your ability to change and grow, and stay committed to your goals. Hope and perseverance inspire ongoing effort and resilience, guiding you towards a brighter future.

As you move forward, remember that recovery is not just about overcoming compulsive behaviors; it's about building a fulfilling and meaningful life. Embrace the journey with courage and determination, knowing that you have the strength to create lasting change and achieve your goals. With the right tools, techniques, and support, you can overcome the challenges posed by compulsive behaviors and work towards a healthier, more balanced, and fulfilling future.

Don't miss out!

Visit the website below and you can sign up to receive emails whenever Timothy Scott Phillips publishes a new book. There's no charge and no obligation.

https://books2read.com/r/B-A-KCQWC-BEEJF

BOOKS 2 READ

Connecting independent readers to independent writers.

About the Author

Timothy Scott Phillips is a dedicated author specializing in non-fiction self-help books that empower readers to overcome challenges and embrace personal growth. With a passion for mental health, resilience, and self-improvement, Timothy combines research-based insights with practical strategies to inspire lasting change. His work reflects a deep commitment to helping individuals navigate life's complexities, build confidence, and unlock their full potential. When he's not writing, Timothy enjoys mentoring, exploring nature, and connecting with his readers to share stories of transformation and hope. His books are a testament to the power of perseverance and the human spirit.

www.ingramcontent.com/pod-product-compliance
Lightning Source LLC
LaVergne TN
LVHW041218150826
845673LV00001B/446

9798230164968